THE PRESIDENT
AND CIVIL RIGHTS

St. Martin's Series
in American Politics

———

Stephen K. Bailey CONGRESS IN THE SEVENTIES
George Kateb POLITICAL THEORY
Grant McConnell THE MODERN PRESIDENCY
Allan P. Sindler POLITICAL PARTIES IN THE UNITED STATES
David G. Smith THE CONVENTION AND THE CONSTITUTION

THE
PRESIDENT
AND
CIVIL RIGHTS

Policy-Making

by Executive Order

RUTH P. MORGAN
Southern Methodist University

ST. MARTIN'S PRESS · NEW YORK

Preface

This book analyzes civil rights policy-making by five modern Presidents: Franklin D. Roosevelt, Harry S. Truman, Dwight D. Eisenhower, John F. Kennedy, and Lyndon B. Johnson. Policy-making by Chief Executives has certainly received its share of attention from social scientists and journalists, but they have focused mainly on foreign policy-making, Presidential leadership in legislation, and executive responsibility for "filling in the details" of congressional statutes. Yet under his independent constitutional authority, the President also on occasion proclaims a policy and orders subordinates to perform certain tasks in order to implement the policy. Few recent books note this policy-making role, although many acknowledge the expansion of Presidential policy-making functions.

The growing power of the Presidency in domestic matters makes the Executive order potentially one of the most significant sources of public law. The democratic theory of government places primary emphasis on the legislature as the lawmaking body, but in the twentieth century Congress was the last to act on civil rights. The first was President Roosevelt, who by Executive order in 1941 proclaimed a nondiscriminatory employment policy for defense industries and established the Fair Employment Practice Committee to implement it. This order was issued thirteen years before the Supreme Court's landmark decision in the School Segregation Cases in 1954 and 1955, and sixteen years before Congress passed the Civil Rights Act of 1957—the first civil rights statute of the twentieth century.

In my analysis of Presidential policy-making by Executive order, I have used a case method and have observed certain restrictions. The scope of the study is limited to civil rights policies which were selected as samples for several reasons. For one, if any reader doubts that the Executive order can be used significantly, the crucial issue of race relations ought to convince him. Furthermore, because the issues are controversial, these cases show most of the complexities of policy-making by Executive order—the interactions of the President, Congress, administrative agencies, special-interest groups, and voters. Even so, the role of one important institution is missing in these cases, since the President's power to establish these particular civil rights policies has not been challenged in the courts.

Case studies of congressional action on civil rights matters are available, which makes it possible to compare policy-making by Executive order with policy-making by statute. Excellent studies of the role of the judicial branch of the government in civil rights matters are also available for comparison. Some of these works are described in the Bibliography under *Civil Rights.*

My study focuses on the rise and fall of policy-making by Executive order in the field of civil rights that took place entirely within a period of three decades. The most important of the orders discussed are listed in the Appendix. Executive Order No. 8802, issued by President Roosevelt in 1941, was the first Executive order on civil rights. Although President Kennedy's fair housing order of 1962 was the last major new civil rights policy established by Executive order, I have included the Johnson administration in order to demonstrate that the Executive order is no longer needed for policy-making when proponents of particular policies succeed in having their measures enacted as statutes.

Certain questions are raised by this method of Presidential action. Why does a President try to bring about change by Executive order? What are the alternative methods? Is the Executive order an effective instrument of policy innovation? What are its implications for the American political system? This is not a comprehensive study of the Executive policy-making process, but instead a description of one aspect of that process—application of Presidential power in specific instances through the instrument of the Executive order, thereby making law. Nevertheless, this dimension of Presidential power also illuminates the broader subject of executive-congressional conflict and cooperation in lawmaking, and it demonstrates the ingenious complexity of the American governmental process.

The constitutional framework, the general nature of the Executive order, and the President's authority to issue them will be considered in the first chapter. This will establish the context for the case studies of equality of treatment and opportunity in the armed services (Chapter II), fair employment practices in government and in private enterprise under government contracts (Chapter III), and equal opportunity in housing (Chapter IV). The final chapter summarizes the conclusions and makes a tentative assessment of the potential of this instrument for policy-making.

For opportunities to make this study, I thank several sources of support. Grants were awarded by the Alpha Gamma Delta Founders Memorial Fund, the Harry S. Truman Library Institute, the Council on Research at Louisiana State University, and the Shell Assists Fund of Southern Methodist University.

Helpful suggestions on an earlier draft came from Dr. Allan R. Richards and Dr. Ronald F. Bunn. The staffs at the Harry S. Truman and Dwight D. Eisenhower Libraries were most helpful and gracious. I owe a special debt to my husband, Vernon, and son, Glenn, who contributed immeasurably to this project through their cooperation and good humor.

Contents

THE PRESIDENT
AND CIVIL RIGHTS

INTRODUCTION

The growth in importance of the Presidency is a distinctive characteristic of our political system as America enters the last third of the twentieth century. Some observers are alarmed by this development; others find it a reason for hope. To the pessimists the expansion of Presidential policy-making functions is one manifestation of a trend that threatens to subvert the principle of separation of powers under the Constitution.

But the framers of the Constitution also incorporated provisions for checks and balances that prevent runaway Executive action. Therefore a proper study of Presidential policy-making must pay some attention to Congress. The two branches are interdependent and important to each other in the lawmaking process.

As policy-makers, Congress and the President are similar, as well as different, in important ways. Each is popularly elected and must return periodically to the voters for their review of performance. Each gives pressure groups access to the policy-making processes. But they represent different constituencies—the President a national one and Congress a state and local one. This has in turn had a substantive effect on national policies. In the field of civil rights, for decades a coalition of conservative Republicans and Southern Democratic Representatives and Senators effectively used procedural complications to stymie legislation. The President, with a more liberal constituency and a national interest, has been more sympathetic to those persons who have been left out by the pattern of effective representation in Congress.

Congress is only one of the factors that affect a President's decisions. The President's own values and his own view of his responsibility to represent all of the people shape his actions, and his judgment of how the courts will rule, and how the administrative agencies that may be charged with enforcing his decisions will react, are important considerations. The President must also weigh the probable reaction of the general public, acting as voters or as members of interest groups.

Much has been written about how decisions are made by the President. So many active participants within the executive branch assist the Chief Executive that a Presidential pronouncement is like the most obvious part of an iceberg. Some participants in the Executive Office are in view above the water line, but most of the work is done by persons out of sight, who have been called the "invisible presidency." This book does not attempt to identify all participants. For no matter who helps to define the problem, to make the recommendations, or to draft the policy statements, not until the President signs the Executive order is a decision binding on the entire nation.

An executive order, of course, is not the final step in the establishment of a policy. Much depends upon how it is interpreted and applied. Great fanfare may surround the ordering of a policy that soon dies for lack of enforcement. As they were carried out, the policies established by these Executive orders did not radically change the lives of Negroes in this country. But the effort to enforce them did in large measure satisfy the civil rights groups without creating an outcry of opposition from other segments of the President's constituency.

If these orders had had little real effect, there would be little need to study this manner in which the President exercises power. But the contrary has been true. About 10 percent of the total work force of the United States was directly affected by the orders concerning military and civilian governmental personnel. Millions more were covered by the provisions in government contracts concerning employment practices. And the fair housing order banned discrimination in about 25 percent of the nation's housing.

Perhaps more significant than even the large number of persons who were directly covered is what Samuel Krislov has called the "multiplier" effect.[1] By this he means that small alterations in governmental policy can instigate changes in a wide arena. Many businesses, for example, voluntarily followed the national government in adopting standards of fair employment practices. In the ban on housing discrimination, civil rights leaders applauded it for its moral effect.

Furthermore, these Presidential policies were the vanguards of new laws governing civil rights. Several years after these Presidential orders, Congress legislated on the same subjects. Not only did the Executive orders provide law during the interval, but also they probably hastened congressional action. When Congress did pass the Civil Rights Acts of 1964 and 1968, it extended the ban on discrimination to the greater part of the nation's work force and to most of the nation's housing. The fact that Congress endorsed these policies and enlarged their coverage testifies to their success.

Finally, one must acknowledge that to determine why a President makes the choices he does is an uncertain enterprise. Truman said that "no one can know all the processes and stages of [a President's] thinking in making important decisions. Even those closest to him . . . never know all the reasons why he does certain things and why he comes to certain conclusions."[2] At times, no doubt, the forces that result in decision are mysterious even to the President himself. Nevertheless, even without complete specific information, one can draw inferences from the record in the attempt to determine why Presidents pursue significant national policy goals by using the Executive order rather than alternative methods.

Certain terms that are used in the following chapters need clarification. In other contexts the word "policy" can mean a variety of things. Here it simply signifies the formal and legally binding statements of public objectives as broad rules applicable to all persons and activities within their compass. "Congressional action" is used to mean committee hearings, committee reporting of a bill, floor debate, and voting. The introduction of a bill and referral to committee is not considered "action." The term "Executive order" is used by some writers to refer to every Presidential act authorizing or directing that an act be performed. Here it designates the proclamations of policy and directions to subordinates that are made by the President in the form of a legally binding Presidential document entitled "Executive Order."

"Nondiscrimination," "equality of treatment and opportunity," "fair employment practices," and "fair housing" are terms which are used to mean that no individual is treated differently from another on the basis of race, color, religion, or national origin. Some people have interpreted the word "nondiscrimination" as meaning "separate but equal." Here "segregation" is used to indicate one manifestation of discrimination.

Chapter I

LEGAL BASIS
OF EXECUTIVE ORDERS

Americans usually think of the President's function under the constitutional doctrine of separation of powers as one of executing the laws that Congress has passed. This view, combined with a strong tradition of mistrust of executive power, engenders cries of "Encroachment!" during the administrations of activist Presidents. Some critics view the issuance of Executive orders independently of an explicit command of Congress as an example of the President overstepping the proper bounds of separation of powers. Such orders "look more like legislation to me than properly authorized regulations to carry out a clear and explicit command of Congress," observed Hugo L. Black, Associate Justice of the U.S. Supreme Court and former U.S. Senator. "And of course," he added, "the Constitution does not confer lawmaking power on the President."[1]

Yet policies established by Executive order have the force of law, even if some scholars dispute their status as "law." They prescribe individual and institutional behavior. Their violation causes loss of government benefits, such as a contract, or brings about other sanctions, such as adverse publicity for failure to comply with an order. They can have nationwide effect. The Executive orders on civil rights, which were not issued under congressional authorization, had all these characteristics. What, then, was the President's authority for issuing them?

Constitutional Framework

In the United States all public policy must ultimately be based upon authority derived from the Constitution. The framers of the Constitution believed that the division of power among three branches and the overlapping of functions through checks and balances were the surest ways to prevent tyranny. "No political truth is certainly of greater intrinsic value," James Madison contended, "than that . . . the accumulation of all powers, legislative, executive, and judiciary, in the same hands . . . may justly be pronounced the very definition of tyranny" (*The Federalist*, No. 47).

Traditionally, legislative power is the authority to make or repeal the laws, executive power is power to administer and enforce them, and judicial power is authority to interpret and apply them. The first three articles of the Constitution vest these powers in a Congress, a President, and courts.

On the basis of explicit delegations of power, as well as implicit constitutional authority, Congress enacts laws that incorporate policies. These statutes are in turn the basis for further policy formulated as Presidential orders or as administrative rules and regulations. The Supreme Court, recognizing that the three articles of the Consitution which distribute power do not "divide fields of black and white" and that some legislative power must be delegated if government is to function, has upheld congressional delegations of discretionary power to the executive branch. Indeed, most authority that Presidents exercise to make policy in domestic matters is specifically delegated by Congress. Of the 1,769 Executive orders signed from 1945 through 1965, about 1,474, or 83 percent, were issued under specific statutory authority.

Nevertheless, Presidents throughout the history of the country have also exercised power, legislative in nature, on the basis of the independent grants of authority in the Constitution. The courts have interpreted the President's authority to make policy in matters of foreign relations as being virtually exclusive and without limit. The limits to Presidential prerogative in domestic affairs, however, are not made so clear by court interpretations.

Nature of the Executive Order

No law, not even an Executive order, defines the term "Executive order." It is not mentioned in the Constitution. In many instances no material difference in style and form exists between Executive orders and other Presidential documents. Since 1945, Title 3 of the *Code of*

Federal Regulations has included the following in the "Presidential documents" category: Executive orders, proclamations, reorganization plans, military orders, regulations, designations of officials (by letter, order, Presidential appointment), interpretations, trade agreement letters, reorganization plans and transfer plans, and administrative orders (including directives, memorandums, letters, notices, designations). But the President's two main formal instruments for promulgating domestic public policy have become, through repeated use, the Executive order and the Presidential proclamation. The courts have recognized no distinction between the two.[2] Emancipation was a proclamation issued by President Lincoln. Since no proclamations have been used to enlarge civil rights in the twentieth century, they are not considered in this book.

The Executive order has not always been recognized as a separate class of Presidential document. The earliest orders are not standardized in form or style. James D. Richardson, who was authorized by Congress to make a compilation of Presidential documents, did not discover Executive orders until after he had completed Volume I in 1895; he corrected this oversight by including them in Volume II, which was published in 1897.

The inauguration of a numbering system around 1907 eliminated most of the confusion as to whether or not a document is an Executive order. All Executive orders on file at the time in the Department of State were arranged chronologically and given a number. Back orders, as they were added to this file, were assigned intermediate numbers.[3] The Executive order officially designated "Number 1" was issued by President Lincoln on October 20, 1862, and concerned the establishment of military courts in Louisiana. An order dated March 10, 1862, ordering deserters from the armed forces to return to duty appears as No. 1 in the *U.S. Statutes at Large,* 1863, although it is not included in the official numbered series.

Since 1929 Presidents have made an effort to coordinate Executive orders through interagency channels and to standardize their style. Nevertheless, there is no required form. And apparently to his surprise, Justice Black found President Truman's steel seizure order to be in a form like that of a statute. He observed that the preamble of the order, like those of many statutes, set out reasons why the President believed certain policies should be adopted. Next, he noted, the policies were proclaimed as rules of conduct to be followed, and again like a statute, the order authorized a government official to make additional rules necessary to carry those policies into execution.[4]

The only statute that governs Executive orders is primarily a notice and publication statute. The Federal Register Act of 1935 requires that

Executive orders "except such as have no general applicability and legal effect" be published in a serial publication, the *Federal Register*. Subsequently, Executive Order No. 10006, issued in 1948, required that all Executive orders be published in the *Federal Register*. In addition, Executive orders may be conveniently found in Title 3 of the *Code of Federal Regulations*.

The Federal Register Act of 1935 also specifies that the contents of the *Federal Register* be judicially noticed. This reinforced an earlier Supreme Court ruling that Executive orders are "public acts of which all courts of the United States are bound to take notice, and to which all courts are bound to give effect."[5]

The Supreme Court also has ruled that Executive orders have "the force of public law,"[6] and that the violation of provisions of an Executive order may be made a crime punishable by sanctions and penalties, if Congress so provides.[7] Even though the President may not define crimes, there are sanctions—such as the refusal of benefits and punitive publicity—that may be imposed without court action.

The constitutionality of particular Executive orders poses a more difficult problem than the judicial review of statutes. While a statute may be held unconstitutional only if it contravenes some provision of the Constitution, an Executive order is held invalid if it conflicts with provisions either of the Constitution or of a statute,[8] or even with the implied intent of Congress.[9] The invalidation of an order found to conflict with a statute has occurred even in an area where the President has a special constitutional status, such as Commander in Chief.[10]

On the other hand, Congress may "ratify" by statute a prior Executive order either by making direct reference to it[11] or by implication. For example, when Congress appropriates funds to support the activity authorized by an Executive order, that action "stands as confirmation and ratification of the action of the Chief Executive."[12] Furthermore, when an Executive practice has been pursued for a long period of time and Congress has known about it and has not objected, the Court accepts Congress's inaction as implicit ratification.[13]

The courts have exercised restraint in ruling on questions of the constitutionality of Presidential actions, and they have generally exempted themselves from jurisdiction over such questions on the grounds that the challenged action is a "political question." Nor does the Supreme Court claim any authority to direct Presidential acts.[14] In cases where the enforcement of an Executive order infringes upon private rights, the limited value of judicial review is also apparent. As with many other matters that are taken to court, it is extremely difficult for the citizen to obtain a judicial ruling quickly enough to remedy a particular injustice arising from an Executive order.

Presidential Powers

Since an Executive order is an exercise of Presidential authority under either the Constitution or a statute, the nature and limitations of Executive power under Article II of the Constitution are a fundamental point at issue. Because Article II is a mere outline of Presidential authority, what powers it vests in the President, to be exercised by him on his own initiative, are more difficult to define than those powers entrusted to him by statute.

Presidential and judicial interpretations of Article II have favored a "broad" construction of the Constitution and have added to the reservoir of constitutional powers which the President can exercise. These powers at times have been called "inherent," "implied," "aggregate," "incidental," "war," and "emergency" powers. The provisions of Article II that have supported claims of broad Presidential authority include the clauses that the "executive Power shall be vested in a President of the United States of America," that the "President shall be Commander in Chief of the Army and Navy of the United States," and that "he shall take Care that the Laws be faithfully executed."

One view of the "executive power" clause is that it adds nothing to Presidential authority but rather is a summary of the powers which Article II proceeds to specify. The other view, however, is that the clause is a grant of general executive power. The "power" theory has been predominant in the views and practices of recent Presidents.

The President's power as Commander in Chief has been transformed from a simple power of military command to one of indeterminable powers in time of emergency. Hamilton believed that this power "would amount to nothing more than the supreme command and direction of the military and naval forces, as first General and Admiral of the Confederacy" (*Federalist*, No. 69). The full import of the Commander in Chief clause was not realized until President Lincoln used both it and the "take care" clause to derive what he termed the "war power." On this basis in a message to Congress he justified the series of measures that he took in the interval between the fall of Fort Sumter, April 14, 1861, and the convening of Congess in a special session on July 4, 1861. The Supreme Court sustained his interpretation of Presidential power in 1863 in the Prize Cases. Subsequently, especially while the war was still in progress, the Court continued to be reluctant to decide against Lincoln in cases involving his "war powers."

With "total war" came Presidential claims of "emergency powers" to justify the use of unusual measures to meet crises. The term "emergency" is not mentioned in the Constitution, but Presidential actions based upon a broad interpretation of constitutional provisions, and the Supreme Court's typical restraint where the Presidency is involved, have permitted a considerable expansion of governmental activity during the past thirty years.

From the clause "he shall take Care that the Laws be faithfully executed," the President derives his role as Chief Administrator. This provision has also been argued along two different lines through the years. One view is that the clause requires the President to carry out the laws of Congress; the other is that the clause is an independent grant of authority. In the Court opinion in the Steel Seizure Case, Justice Black expressed the restrictive view, saying, "The President's power to see that the laws are faithfully executed refutes the idea that he is to be a lawmaker." Black argued that "the Constitution limits his functions in the lawmaking process to the recommending of laws he thinks wise and the vetoing of laws he thinks bad."

On the other hand, a Supreme Court decision in 1899 interpreted this clause as a grant of authority to make policy. Justice Miller, writing for the Court, said that the President's constitutional duty to "take care that the laws be faithfully executed" is not "limited to the enforcement of acts of Congress or of treaties according to their express terms," but includes "the rights, duties, and obligations growing out of the Constitution itself . . . and all the protection implied by the nature of the government under the Constitution."[15] Presidents have claimed broad powers under this clause on many occasions.

Under the view that the "executive power" and "take care" clauses grant power, Presidents Roosevelt, Truman, Eisenhower, Kennedy, and Johnson issued Executive orders prohibiting discrimination in government employment, in private enterprise under government contract, and in federally assisted housing. The Commander in Chief clause provided the basis for the Presidential ban on segregation in the armed forces.

Chapter II

EQUALITY IN
THE ARMED SERVICES

"There are no longer any all-Negro units in the Services." With these words a progress report, issued January 1, 1955, by the Defense Department, told of a significant change in the U.S. armed forces.[1] On July 26, 1948, President Truman had issued Executive Order No. 9981, which declared the policy of the nation to be "equality of treatment and opportunity for all persons in the armed services without regard to race, color, religion, or national origin." The order also established a Committee on Equality of Treatment and Opportunity in the Armed Services to make recommendations for carrying out the new policy. Most of the people concerned about the racial policies of the military service considered the major step in eliminating discrimination to be desegregation of the armed forces.

Background of a Presidential Decision

Presidents make decisions in a political environment that encompasses not only present conditions but also past experiences. A review of personnel policies as they relate to discrimination in the armed services prior to 1948 reveals that President Truman reinforced an emerging trend when he issued an Executive order directing equal treatment. It speeded up a process already under way in the Navy, and beginning in the Air Force and Army.

Congress had already indicated intent in one instance: the Selective Service Act of 1940 stipulated that in the selection and training of men under the Act there should be no discrimination against any person on account of race or color. This provision had been introduced as an amendment by Representative Hamilton Fish on behalf of the Committee on Participation of Negroes in the War, a group established by a Negro newspaper, the *Pittsburgh Courier.* The Committee believed the amendment would abolish segregation in the armed forces. It didn't.

A spokesman for the NAACP said several years later that the nondiscrimination clause in the Selective Service Act of 1940 had meant nothing. Truman K. Gibson, Negro civilian aide to Secretary of War Stimson, disagreed. He contended that if the amendment had not been inserted in the law, the Army might have chosen the easy way out of a difficult problem and simply not taken the number of Negroes that it did during World War II.[2]

In actual practice, policies with regard to racial segregation in the armed services depended upon the will of the officers administering particular programs. Some men at various echelons prodded the services into allowing greater opportunities for Negroes, while other officers who were more tradition-bound resisted such efforts.

Although the Selective Service Act included a nondiscrimination clause, the White House on October 9, 1940, released a War Department statement announcing that Negro personnel would be substantially increased so as to constitute the same proportion in the Army as in the national population, but that the War Department would maintain segregated regiments. Furthermore, the all-Negro 92d and 93d Divisions were reactivated in World War II, contrary to the assurance the Army gave Selective Service that Negro divisions would not be formed.[3]

Despite the Army's segregation policy throughout the war, the need for combat troops in Europe in 1945 caused a dent in segregation practices. Negro platoons were assigned among eleven combat divisions of the First and Seventh Armies. At that time Negro soldiers would have been used in completely unsegregated combat units if the War Department had not objected. After V-E Day, most of these platoons were ordered out of the combat divisions and assigned once more to service units.

In late 1945 the Army convened a special board of general officers, headed by Lieutenant General Alvan C. Gillem, Jr., to submit recommendations on racial policy to the Secretary of War and the Chief of

Staff. The Army had decided, on the basis of reports by field commanders throughout the war and a thorough staff and field study, that its racial policies had proved unsatisfactory.[4]

The Gillem Board concluded that segregation should be maintained, but that the Army had to expand the number of jobs in which Negroes could serve. The report recommended eliminating the all-Negro Army division and including a minority race unit in every larger Army unit. However, the minority race unit would be housed in separate barracks and have its own mess facilities.[5] The War Department approved these recommendations, and the Army was operating under Gillem policy when Truman issued Executive Order No. 9981. Nevertheless, the Army had taken the step of adopting an educational program to win tolerance for Negro troops.[6]

During World War II the Air Force, since it was a part of the Army, had the same racial policy as the Army—i.e., a 10 percent Negro enlisted strength restriction, segregated units, and greatly limited job opportunities. Following the war, before the Air Force was made a separate department, a number of Air Force staff memoranda recommended that Negro airmen, like white ones, be used solely on the basis of their individual qualifications, and that no Air Force jobs carry a racial restriction. However, the same memoranda insisted that segregation must be maintained because of social customs and possible difficulties if Negro and white airmen were placed in the same unit.[7]

W. Stuart Symington became the first Secretary of the independent Air Force in September, 1947. Symington was known for progressive labor and race relations views, which he had quietly implemented at his industrial plant, the Emerson Electric Manufacturing Company in St. Louis. Walter White, long-time executive secretary of the NAACP, found him equally firm and sincere in his determination to achieve racial integration in the Air Force.[8] Symington had taken some preliminary steps toward that goal when President Truman issued Order 9981.

By 1948, the Navy also was beginning to make progress in implementing a policy of nondiscrimination. Frank Knox, Secretary of the Navy until 1944, had bitterly resisted efforts to change the status of Negroes. When the 1940 Selective Service Act passed, Knox announced that Negroes could not be accepted in any other capacity than as mess attendants.[9] Since the Navy then relied on voluntary recruitment, it was able to pursue this discriminatory policy for a time. Following several memoranda from President Roosevelt, however, the Navy began enlisting some Negroes in general service after June 1, 1942. In February, 1943, under a Presidential directive, the Navy began to receive its manpower through Selective Service, and at the same time the War Manpower Commission insisted that the Navy accept Negroes in the same proportion as the other branches.[10]

As in the Army, considerations of military efficiency were an important factor in the Navy's reversal of policy. Because of limited billets, the Navy was forced to meet the problem created by racial segregation when Negroes entered in growing numbers in 1943.[11] The Navy created a Special Programs Unit to handle the Negro problem. The first step was to man two small seagoing craft entirely by Negroes. However, the Special Unit soon decided that all-Negro ships were no solution to the Navy's problem, since there were not enough trained Negroes to handle the many jobs on ships. The first real breakthrough came when the Special Unit secured approval to include Negroes, up to a maximum of 10 percent of the crews, with white crew members on twenty-five selected auxiliary ships. This was accomplished by late 1944.

When James Forrestal became Secretary of the Navy after Knox's death in 1944, he received permission from President Roosevelt to change the Navy's racial policies. In 1945 Forrestal assigned Lester B. Granger, executive secretary of the National Urban League, to tour Navy bases and recommend specific action.[12] Moreover, Charles S. Thomas, Secretary of the Navy under Eisenhower, relates that after Mrs. Roosevelt complained to Forrestal that segregation was being practiced to an unreasonable degree in the Navy, he made a tour of some thirty bases in the Pacific at Forrestal's request.[13] Subsequently, on February 27, 1946, the Navy opened all general service assignments to Negroes and ordered that "in the utilization of housing, messing and other facilities, no special or unusual provisions will be made for the accommodation of Negroes."[14]

Between February 27, 1946, and July 26, 1948, when Truman signed Executive Order No. 9981, the Navy issued a series of directives designed to reinforce an integration policy.[15] The President's Committee on Civil Rights noted in 1947, however, that although the Navy had done a good job of verbalizing policy and had "tried fitfully to enforce the policy on certain lower levels," the Navy had only one Negro commissioned officer in contrast to approximately thirteen hundred in the Army. Nevertheless, when Walter White talked with Forrestal in 1948 at President Truman's request, he found him "quietly determined to achieve full integration while he was Secretary of the Navy."[16]

Pressures for Policy Changes

Seizing the opportunity presented by Presidential emergency powers during World War II, the leaders of civil rights organizations put pressure on the executive branch to meet their demands. Two weeks after President Roosevelt had signed the Selective Service Act of 1940, a delegation that included A. Philip Randolph, Brotherhood of Sleeping Car Porters, and Walter White, executive secretary of the NAACP, conferred with him to discuss discrimination against the Negro in the armed services and defense industries. The Negro leaders submitted a seven-point program for abolishing segregation in the military. When no action resulted, and after fruitless requests to see the President again, Randolph originated the idea of a march on Washington, set for July 1, 1941.

Responding to this threat of a large demonstration, President Roosevelt again received a delegation that included Randolph, who requested that the President issue an Executive order to end discrimination in war industries and the armed services.[17] The President did establish the Committee on Fair Employment Practice by Executive Order No. 8802, June 25, 1941, and the march on Washington was called off. But he did not issue an order desegregating the armed forces.

In 1944, civil rights organizations exerted pressure to secure favorable platform promises from the major parties. Delegates from twenty-five Negro organizations, with an estimated six and a half million members, met in New York on June 17, 1944, to formulate a statement of Negro demands. This stipulated that political parties and candidates seeking the Negro vote be committed to ending the segregation of Negroes in the armed forces.[18] The Democrats did put a general statement on civil rights into their 1944 platform, but the Republicans went farther. They pledged an immediate congressional inquiry to ascertain the extent to which mistreatment, segregation, and discrimination against Negroes in the armed forces impaired morale and efficiency. The Republican platform also promised subsequent corrective legislation.

Following World War II, civil rights organizations continued to put pressure on the President and the military authorities to desegregate the armed forces. After Truman assumed office, a delegation of six civil rights leaders met with him on September 19, 1945. These were James B. Carey, secretary of the CIO; Boris Shishkin of the AFL; Dr. Herman Reissig, Federal Council of the Churches of Christ in America; Dr. Channing H. Tobias, director of the Phelps-Stokes Fund; Leslie Perry, administrative assistant in the Washington office of the NAACP; and Walter White of the NAACP.[19]

White, the delegation's spokesman, recounts that the "President sat quietly, elbows resting on the arms of his chair and his fingers interlocked against his stomach as he listened with a grim face to the story of the lynchings in Georgia and Louisiana, the flood of viciously anti-Semitic, anti-Catholic, anti-labor, and anti-foreign-born literature with which more than sixty hate organizations were inundating the country." White says that when he had finished, the President exclaimed, "My God! I had no idea it was as terrible as that! We've got to do something!"[20]

President Truman decided to create a President's Committee on

Civil Rights by Executive Order No. 9808, and to it he appointed Carey, Shishkin, and Tobias. The Committee's subsequent report, *To Secure These Rights,* provided the basis for the President's ten-point civil rights program, presented in a special message to Congress on February 2, 1948.

A civil rights delegation conferred with the President again in March. At this time Grant Reynolds, chairman of the Committee Against Jim Crow in Military Service and Training, presented seven proposals for eliminating segregation in the armed forces. He warned Truman that mass civil disobedience would result if the draft law did not include antisegregation provisions.[21] The President gave Reynolds no assurance that he would change the existing policy, and he indicated that the proposals should be enacted by Congress and not left to administrative bodies.[22]

Reynolds also presented his proposals and repeated his threat of mass civil disobedience at House and Senate hearings on selective service and universal military training in 1948. In addition, representatives of the National Youth Assembly against Military Training, the National Association for the Advancement of Colored People, the Committee to Abolish Segregation from the Universal Military Training Program, and the Americans for Democratic Action testified against segregation in the armed services.

American Negroes also took their grievances to the United Nations. In 1946 the National Negro Congress petitioned the Economic and Social Council to use its influence to eliminate discrimination in the United States. The following year the National Association for the Advancement of Colored People presented an annotated 154-page document to the United Nations Department of Social Affairs. The Association did not expect that the petition would have immediate results. Rather, it hoped to influence public opinion on a national and international scale in order to improve the status of the American Negro.[23]

The President was influenced to some extent by the effect that segregation practices in the United States armed forces had upon world opinion. He suggested in his memoirs that any other course than integration in the armed services would have been inconsistent with international commitments and obligations. "We could not endorse a color line at home and still expect to influence the immense masses that make up the Asian and African peoples," Truman wrote.[24]

Action in Congress

Armed services desegregation did not become an important legislative issue until the 80th Congress's long battle over the armed forces manpower program in 1948. Many organizations felt that a fight should be made at that time for including a nonsegregation clause in the bill.[25] Indeed, the principal battles on the manpower bill in both houses concerned segregation amendments.

Organizations interested in the nonsegregation clause, such as the Committee Against Jim Crow in Military Service and Training, threatened political reprisal and mass civil disobedience if segregation were not eliminated in the armed services. The National Association for the Advancement of Colored People had supported the 1940 Selective Training and Service Act. In 1948 the board of directors formally opposed compulsory training "both because it is generally unsound in principle and the present legislation would permit the continuation of the present racial segregation and discrimination in the armed forces."[26]

Certain developments in the Senate Armed Services Committee caused great concern among the backers of the draft program. When Senator William Langer, Republican of North Dakota, tried unsuccessfully to get the Committee to accept seven antisegregation amendments, he served notice that he would force to a vote on the floor of the Senate a proposal to incorporate virtually all of President Truman's civil rights program into the bill.[27] On the other hand, just before the committee vote on the bill, Senator Richard B. Russell, Democrat of Georgia, proposed an amendment to give each draftee the right to say that he preferred service in a unit of his own race. The committee rejected the amendment 4 to 7.[28] This defeat, according to Russell, was "because of the assurances we received from those in positions of high authority that they did not intend to prosecute this program [of integration]."[29] President Truman, however, responding to a question at his May 28 news conference, stated that the injection of the segregation issue into the congressional fight had not caused any change in his instructions to the Secretary of Defense to eliminate discrimination within the armed forces. The President made no distinction between racial "discrimination" and "segregation," a fact which bothered Negro leaders. Negroes considered segregation per se to be evidence of discrimination; they did not believe that "separate but equal" could be nondiscriminatory.

When Langer, as he had promised, offered his seven amendments from the floor on June 7, the Senate showed little inclination to tie the question of armed forces desegregation to the draft question. Calls to stop debate were responded to without noticeable protest; three times the Senate approved motions to shelve the pending question and thus end discussion. The Senate rejected six of the seven amendments, but in a surprise move, by a vote of 37 to 35, adopted the Langer proposal that a poll tax imposed on servicemen voting in federal elections be suspended for the duration of the draft act. It had been forecast that the

Republicans would move to inject some concrete achievement into that session's admittedly almost blank performance on civil rights, and the poll tax vote seemed to be confirmation.[30] The vote on another Langer amendment, the one to prohibit racial segregation in the armed forces, had been construed earlier as one that might test the "Solid South" resistance. Nevertheless, the amendment was tabled by a 67 to 7 roll call vote.

While Senator Langer wished to amend the Selective Service Bill because "this is the only chance left before we adjourn for carrying out our [Republican platform] promises," the Southern Senators made it clear that they would attempt to write a segregation clause into the bill. Unable to get the Armed Services Committee to accept the "voluntary segregation" amendment, Senators Russell and Burnet R. Maybank, Democrat of South Carolina, offered it on the Senate floor after the night session on Langer's amendment. In advancing his proposal, Russell alerted the Senate to the possibility of Presidential action by Executive order. He pointed out that on the eve of an election "an administration would be subjected to great pressure if it were compelled, because of the failure to abolish segregation in the armed services, to face the threat of mass civil disobedience affecting three or four hundred thousand men and perhaps one million or more votes." He contended that it would certainly be a temptation for the President to yield rather than to be confronted with mass prosecutions all over the United States.

However, the Russell-Maybank amendment was rejected by voice vote on June 9, and the Senate overwhelmingly adopted the Selective Service Bill. The House action on it immediately bogged down in a civil rights conflict. House leaders had hoped the measure would pass quickly, but they abandoned this idea after antidiscrimination and antisegregation amendments were offered by Jacob K. Javits, Republican of New York, by Adam Clayton Powell, Jr., Democrat of New York, and two days later, by Leo Isacson, American Labor Party of New York. All three of these amendments were rejected by margins of more than 65 votes. John Bell Williams, Democrat of Mississippi, offered an amendment similar to Senator Russell's. This was rejected 88 to 24. The House finally approved the bill on June 18, 1948.

Presidential Action

President Truman outlined his civil rights program in a special message to Congress on February 2, 1948. He did not request legislative action to desegregate the armed services, as the President's Committee on Civil Rights had proposed. This course was recommended by Stephen J. Spingarn—son of a former president of the NAACP and at the time assistant general counsel in the Treasury Department— and members of the President's staff. Spingarn was detailed to the White House in mid-January to assist Clark Clifford, special counsel to the President, in preparing legislation to carry out the recommendations that would be made by the President in the civil rights message. In addition to Clifford and Spingarn, Robert Carr, George M. Elsey, Charles Murphy, and Philleo Nash participated in the drafting sessions, and they considered legislation to end racial segregation in the armed forces unnecessary. They decided that Clifford should discuss administrative action with Forrestal and then include a reference to future action in the message to Congress.[31]

The President announced in this message that he would "shortly issue an Executive Order containing a comprehensive restatement of the Federal nondiscrimination policy, together with appropriate measures to ensure compliance." However, he did indicate the decision to use less formal means for dealing with segregation in the armed forces, for he went on to say that he had instructed the Secretary of Defense to have the remaining instances of discrimination eliminated as rapidly as possible.

On May 11, 1948, the Secretaries of Defense, the Army, the Navy, and the Air Force met with members of the White House staff to decide on the means for implementing the relevant passages of the President's civil rights message. At that time they favored creating a Board on Troop Policy in the Office of the Secretary of Defense.[32] Thus, at least as late as May 11, 1948, the President did not intend to issue an Executive order, but rather meant to press for the gradual desegregation of the armed services in the departments.

What occurred between May 11 and July 26 to prompt the President to issue Executive Order No. 9981? As discussed in the previous section, armed forces desegregation became an important point of conflict in the congressional controversy over a new draft law. The conflict was politically charged, since Langer proposed amendments in a move to fulfill Republican platform promises, and Russell, who offered the segregation amendment, was up for reelection.

Also, in the interim the Democratic Party held its national convention in Philadelphia July 12–14. In a move to keep the South from bolting, Truman supporters backed a general civil rights plank that had the advantage of not committing the party to the specific ten-point program President Truman had urged on Congress, while it still subscribed to his goal of equal opportunity and security under the law for all Americans. After the moderate plank was reported to the convention by the Resolutions (Platform) Committee, an amendment reasserting the principle of states' rights was offered by the Southern delegations, but is was overwhelmingly defeated. Then Minneapolis Mayor Hubert H. Humphrey, vice chairman of Americans for Democratic Action and a member of the Resolutions Committee, seized the opportunity to offer a specific plank supporting the President's program. He and other party liberals demanded that four of the objectives of the President's civil rights program be spelled out in the platform, and their proposal won by a 651½ to 582½ vote. One of the four points in the amended plank was "the right of equal treatment in the service and defense of our nation." The others were abolition of poll taxes in federal elections and antilynching and fair employment practices legislation.

The adoption of the floor amendment on civil rights was followed by a walkout of the Mississippi and Alabama delegations. On July 17, Southerners from thirteen states convened in Birmingham, Alabama, to nominate J. Strom Thurmond, governor of South Carolina, as the presidential candidate of the States' Rights (Dixiecrat) Party. In the election Truman was to lose the votes of Alabama, Louisiana, Mississippi, and South Carolina to this party.

At 2 A.M. on July 15 at the Democratic convention, Harry S. Truman made an acceptance speech in which he castigated the Republicans for their "rich-man's" programs and criticized the "do-nothing Republican 80th Congress." Toward the end of the speech he caused the first surprise of his campaign by announcing that he was going to call Congress back into session on July 26 and ask it to pass the legislation that Republicans advocated, including civil rights measures. Truman recorded in his memoirs that he knew the special session would produce no results in the way of legislation, but that he felt justified in calling Congress back to Washington to prove that the Republicans "would run out on their platform."[33]

The *New York Times* reported that Truman had decided to recall Congress at least a week before his acceptance speech.[34] The President resolved later, probably after the convention had amended the party platform's civil rights plank, to issue Executive Order No. 9981 and the companion order, No. 9980. In this way he could show that he would act with regard to civil rights when the Republicans would not.

Oscar R. Ewing, Federal Security Administrator, backed Truman's position as a political imperative and felt that the orders did play a part in the election.[35] After the convention, Ewing advised the President that he must immediately do everything within his power as Chief Executive to carry out the civil rights provisions of the Democratic platform, or the Democrats would lose the Negro vote. "There was never a question where Truman stood," Ewing stated later. "Any question he had was how far he could go."

Philip Nash, Clark Clifford, Ewing, and others drafted the orders. Nash urged the creation of a committee within the military establishment to push steps toward desegregation, with Presidential appointees as members to give it stature and authority. "Let the committee find out in each branch where segregation hurts efficiency," he advised. "Don't spell it out in advance."

Oscar R. Ewing took the proposed Executive order to Forrestal for military clearance. Forrestal, according to Max Leva, who was then his special assistant, urged that the order call for progress "as rapidly as feasible," rather than lay down any flat edict. He believed that this approach would give the services an opportunity to work out methods of compliance, rather than arousing their antagonism.

Forrestal also said he was certain there would be no objection from Symington or Secretary of the Navy Sullivan, but he asked Ewing to discuss the proposed order with Kenneth C. Royall, Secretary of the Army.[36] Royall was known to be reluctant to change segregation practices. For example, the NAACP passed a resolution at its 1948 convention that called for Royall's resignation because of his anti-Negro sentiments and policies. Royall believed that "the question of integration involves a vital problem of social reform to be achieved first by the people of the United States and then by the United States Army." [37]

Nash later commented that "political necessity dictated the timing for steps on which much patient preparation had been made, and provided the opportunity to accomplish the results the President wanted." The role of the equal rights directives in the 1948 election, Nash observed, "shows the importance of politics in making progress toward American ideals. . . . To meet the challenge of the Democratic platform, after a convention fight, required the Chief Executive to take action."[38]

On July 26, the eve of his appearance before the special session of Congress, the President announced his two civil rights Executive orders. One related to fair employment practices within the federal government, and the other related to equality of opportunity and treatment in the armed services.

The announcement provoked little reaction. Most commentators interpreted the order as a politically motivated move and regarded its effect with skepticism. When queried by a *Washington Post* reporter, spokesmen for the armed services were noncommittal.[39] However, one unnamed federal official intimated that it would be a long time before high officers carried integration down to the squad, as this would involve white men and Negroes eating and sleeping in the same quarters. Since the order did not name a deadline for action and did not mention segregation, this official regarded President Truman's action as "a pretty good political approach" that would not too greatly affront Southern Democrats.[40]

Order 9981 followed by less than twenty-four hours the adoption of the Progressive Party platform, which called for "a Presidential proclamation ending segregation and all forms of discrimination in the armed services and Federal employment." Since the Progressive Party's candidate, Henry Wallace, was a major threat to Truman from the left in 1948, Senator Russell charged that the orders were "articles of unconditional surrender to the Wallace convention" as well as to "the treasonable civil disobedience campaign" organized by A. Philip Randolph and Grant Reynolds.[41]

The order, however, did not immediately satisfy Randolph, who labeled it "a misleading move, obviously made for political purposes and deliberately calculated to obscure the issue of segregation and to confuse the people at home and aboard." Randolph again called upon Negro and white youths to refuse to register for the draft unless segregation was abolished in the armed forces.[42] Nevertheless, by September the Negro press had abandoned its campaign against the Army's racial policy, civil rights leaders had pledged to support the committee established by the order, and all important opposition to the draft on the basis of the Army's race policy had disappeared.[43]

Extension of remarks in the *Congressional Record* was light. Only three Congressmen—Ed Gossett of Texas and Overton Brooks and Leonard Allen of Louisiana—commented on the order. They said that it was politically motivated, and Gossett charged that "the President has again surrendered to the Reds and radicals."

Application of the New Policy

The Presidential order offered loopholes for those who might seek them. Besides the lack of a time limit for implementation, it provided a possibility for delaying tactics by stating that the policy was to be effected as rapidly as possible "without impairing efficiency or morale." The Committee on Equality of Treatment and Opportunity in the Armed Services was to be "advisory" to the national military establishment. Therefore, much depended upon the Committee members and their decisions, the attitude of the military command, and the support of the President.

Charles Fahy, former Solicitor General, was appointed Chairman of the Committee. At the first meeting, held January 12, 1949, the President told the Secretaries of the military departments and the Committee that he wanted "a survey of the situation." He said he hoped for a concrete proposition not later than June 1, so that he would have an outline of the situation before Congress adjourned, in case he wanted to ask for amendments to the law.[44]

The Committee decided, however, that the report to the President should represent not a future objective, but a program in being. The Committee believed that reforms would be more readily accepted and make headway faster if they represented decisions mutually agreed upon by the services and the Committee. The President approved this plan, and when the Committee reported to the President on May 22, 1950, the recommendations were already in effect.[45]

The attitude of those in command was a substantial factor in the success of the new Air Force and Navy racial policies. The Air Force, spurred by the President's Executive order, completed its own desegregation plan. Secretary Symington called on Truman and asked, "Mr. President, do you mean this order? Because if you do it's going to be enforced."

"I mean every word of it," answered Truman.[46]

Symington then conferred with all the Air Force generals who were of Southern family or background. He told them he personally believed that the order was for the benefit of the fighting forces, but that even if he did not agree, he would enforce the order of the Commander in Chief to the letter. The Secretary told the generals that if they dissented, he wanted them to say so then. All agreed to comply. Next, Symington asked George Weaver, a Negro official of the International Electricians' Union, to make policy suggestions. Weaver agreed to help.

By November, 1948, the Air Force had framed a policy and a detailed program for putting it into effect within a year. These plans were sent to the President's Committee on Equality of Treatment and Opportunity in the Armed Services for the first meeting in January, 1949. The Committee thought the proposals represented a great advance over existing practice. Nevertheless, it had serious reservations regarding two provisions in the new program—the 10 percent limitation upon Negro strength in any one unit, and the discretion left to commanders to determine whether individual Negroes were best suited for assignment to racial units.[47]

On April 6, 1949, eight months after President Truman issued the Executive order, Secretary of Defense Louis Johnson sent the Secretaries of the three military departments a memorandum reiterating the President's policy and asking them to submit a program by May 1 for carrying it out.[48] In reply, the Air Force resubmitted its earlier proposals in essentially their original form; significantly, however, it omitted the two provisions about which the Committee had expressed reservations.[49] The Secretary of Defense approved this new policy in early May. The Air Force began implementing it on June 1, 1949, and voluntarily submitted periodic progress reports to the Committee.[50] Late in November, six months after orders had gone to the field commanders, Air Force Headquarters notified the Committee that the Air Force was prepared for a thorough field investigation of the results of the new policy. On this inspection trip the Committee's staff found only one segregated unit.[51]

As for the Navy, the Committee found little to criticize in training and assignment practices. It was concerned, however, that the opportunities the Navy offered had not attracted a larger number of Negroes to enlist for general service. The Committee made recommendations designed to increase the number of Negroes in general service, as well as in the Naval Reserve Officers Training Corps program, and to correct the inequality in the Steward's Branch. These proposals were all accepted by the Navy.[52]

The situation in the Army was markedly different from that in the Air Force and Navy. Some of the highest-ranking Army officials maintained that the President's order did not *require* an end to segregation.[53] The Army was slow in responding to Secretary Johnson's April 6 directive, and when it did so Johnson asked that the policy proposals be revised.[54] Finally, on September 30, a press release announced that Secretary Johnson approved the Army's fourth reply to his directive. The new Army proposals included two of the four recommendations that the Fahy Committee had made in May—that all jobs be open to qualified personnel regardless of race and that no racial quota be established for school attendance.[55]

Evidence in the Fahy Committee records indicates that the Army, rather than the Department of Defense, may have issued the September 30 press release regarding Johnson's approval of the new Army policy, and that the Army had conveyed the impression to the Department of Defense that the statement had been approved by the Committee. The press release implied, but avoided stating, that the Fahy Committee had approved the plan.

The Army was equivocal on the Committee's recommendation that the restriction on assignment of Negroes be removed. And with regard to the fourth recommendation, the abolition of the racial quota, Gordon Gray, Secretary of the Army, promised only to continue to study the matter. The Army and the Committee were slow to resolve their differences on these problems. Despite active White House support of the Committee,[56] Chairman Fahy tried to reconcile the differences without drawing the White House, or the public, further into the controversy.[57]

The Committee and the Army, in consultation, finally worked out a policy and procedure on assignment that took into account the number of men involved and the time required to screen, train, and reassign them. As a result of discussions between Fahy, Gray, and General J. Lawton Collins, Army Chief of Staff, the Army issued new instructions on Negro manpower utilization on January 10, 1950.[58] Secretary Gray explained that the new regulations provided for the mandatory transfer of men in the critical specialties and the permissive transfer where an Army commander thought it desirable, but noted that "there is no policy of elimination of segregation in the Army at the present time."[59]

The reconciliation of views on the racial quota was even more troublesome. In January the White House urged Fahy to have the Committee and the Army arrive at a solution to the quota problem as soon as possible. In March the Army finally decided to abolish the quota, but to do so without advance publicity.[60] Apparently some officers in the Army command felt that they would inevitably lose the battle for segregation policies and might as well go ahead and act and get the credit for it.[61] With the Army's abolition of the racial quota in a routine order to field commanders on March 27, 1950, the Committee's principal recommendations to the Army had been accepted.[62]

Although opinions differ on the effect of the President's order, backed by the Fahy Committee's actions, on the Army's racial policies, there is considerable agreement that in any case, the Army would not have moved as speedily toward desegregation had not the Korean War begun in June, 1950. Even then, General Douglas MacArthur refused to use the available Negro troops to their fullest capacity, or to integrate them. Segregation practices continued until General Matthew Ridgway, who requested and received permission to integrate all American troops under his command, replaced General MacArthur.[63]

June 30, 1954, was the scheduled deadline for the abolition of any remaining all-Negro units in the armed forces. By this time Eisenhower had succeeded Truman to the Presidency, but the deadline was met. In a progress report issued January 1, 1955, the Defense Department announced that there were no longer any all-Negro units in the services. President Truman relieved the Committee of its assignment, but left the Executive order in effect, in case it might be desirable at some later date to examine the implementation of the Committee's recommendations.[64]

Although the President's order specifically stated that the new policy was "equality of treatment and opportunity" in the military services, the emphasis in the implementation effort was upon desegregation. This was interpreted as the major step toward nondiscrimination. In this sense, then, the order was implemented within the decade. The success of the desegregation program has been attributed in part to the fact that from the start of concrete planning until around 1952, there was little publicity. According to an Army general staff officer, they feared that stories in the papers would cause Southern Congressmen "to get up on their hind legs and oppose it," and they preferred "to get it done without fanfare and then tell about it."[65]

Subsequent Congressional and Executive Action

Some Southern Congressmen did oppose Order 9981 and the efforts to desegregate the armed forces. In an immediate reaction to the President's announcement, Arthur Winstead, Democrat of Mississippi, introduced a bill in the House "to strengthen the national defense" by making it possible for persons drafted under the Selective Service Act of 1948 to choose the type of units in which they would serve. The bill was referred to committee and no further action was taken.

However, while the President's Committee was working to implement the order, Congress did not let the issue die. Segregation in the armed forces again received serious congressional attention in 1950, when the 81st Congress considered extending the 1948 Selective Service Act. Both the Senate and the House Armed Services Committees held hearings on draft extension and weighed various proposed antisegregation amendments. The Senate committee approved one offered by Richard Russell that was essentially the same "voluntary segregation" proposal rejected by the committee in 1948 and subsequently rejected on the Senate floor. It was rejected again this time on the floor.

Defeat of the Russell plan cleared the way for passage of the draft extension bill. Senator Humphrey decided not to offer the series of antisegregation amendments he had prepared, because he feared a filibuster and felt that the urgency of the situation necessitated draft extension.[66] In the House, however, Representatives Powell and Javits offered antisegregation amendments, charging that the Army had resisted and that the time had come for Congress to act. Both amendments were overwhelmingly defeated.

In the 82d Congress during consideration of the 1951 amendments to the Selective Service Act, Representative Winstead got the House Armed Services Committee, in a closed-door meeting, to accept by a 20 to 11 vote an amendment that would give men the right to choose whether or not they wished to serve in segregated units. The chairman of the committee, Carl Vinson of Georgia, voted against the rider because he said the military leaders were opposed to it.[67] Walter White relates that at considerable expense, delegations were brought to Washington from key states to oppose the Winstead amendment.[68] The Committee voted 32 to 3 to report the bill, but the amendment was eliminated during floor action by a 178 to 126 teller vote.

Representative Adam Clayton Powell, Jr., of New York, introduced his bill to prohibit race segregation in the armed forces for the last time on January 3, 1953. He had presented it to each session of Congress from the 79th through the 83d, but each time it was referred to the Committee on the Armed Services and no further action was taken. Powell also offered an antisegregation amendment to every bill pertaining to the armed forces that came before the House from 1945 until 1954, except during the Korean conflict. On April 29, 1954, he announced on the floor that he could now vote with a clear conscience for appropriations for the armed services since "today, there is not a single segregated arm of our Defense Department."

Subsequent congressional, as well as administrative, activity related to the Negro in the armed services has concentrated on segregation in the National Guard and ROTC, and on equality of opportunity for servicemen and their dependents, both on base and off. Evidence in the

Eisenhower papers points to some continued interest by the President in investigating complaints of segregation or discrimination in the military and in correcting these situations.[69]

President Kennedy continued the effort. In 1962 he established a Committee on Equal Opportunity in the Armed Forces, headed by Gerhard A. Gesell, to determine what further measures might be required. One result of the Committee's initial report to the President was a Defense Department directive in 1963 ordering the military services to issue regulations protecting the civil rights of servicemen on base and off. It allowed a base commander, upon approval by the civilian Secretary of his service, to declare a segregated establishment "off-limits."[70] The directive stirred a storm of protest in Congress, but this dissipated in the following year when Congress passed the Civil Rights Act of 1964, with its public-accommodations provisions. In 1967, commanders were told to seek out landlords and to urge them to rent to all servicemen without regard to color, and to point out that if they refused, no servicemen would be authorized to deal with them. By July, 1968, 84 percent of the landlords throughout the nation were on the Defense Department's nondiscriminatory housing lists.[71]

The final report of the President's Committee on Equal Opportunity in the Armed Forces, which was submitted to President Johnson in late 1964, dealt with the special problems of discrimination faced by servicemen on foreign duty and servicemen in National Guard units. When the President sent a copy of the Committee's report to the Secretary of Defense, Robert S. McNamara, he urged that "every effort be made to continue this movement toward a National Guard in every state in which there will be no barriers against participation based on race, color or creed."[72]

Conclusion

As described in this chapter, the case of desegregation of the armed forces suggests that the President may use the formal Executive order as the means for achieving an objective when it serves a partisan political purpose. President Truman was willing to act affirmatively in the field of civil rights, and also on the specific problem of armed forces segregation, when that issue was forced to his attention by the demands of civil rights groups. The major decision, therefore, became one of choosing between alternative courses of action.

The President's own Committee on Civil Rights recommended legislation to prohibit segregation in the armed services. Why did Truman omit a request for legislation from his 1948 civil rights message to Congress? Competing civil rights priorities and the fact that desegregation of the armed forces could be accomplished administratively were probably the main factors influencing this decision. Nevertheless, the

President might have supported an antisegregation amendment after the issue was injected into the congressional debate over selective service. No doubt he rejected this course because of the overriding necessity to get the Selective Service Act passed.

Another avenue open to the President was the gradual desegregation of the armed services by means of instructions to subordinates and other informal pressures. Truman had apparently chosen this approach at least as late as May 11, 1948. Therefore, it seems apparent that the main reason for switching to the formal Executive order was the political need to provide an asset for the Democrats in the 1948 campaign. Truman knew that the Negro vote could be crucial in the pivotal states, so he changed his course from a low-key informal effort to desegregate the armed services to the Executive order, with its greater status and potential for publicity.

Truman should not be charged with issuing the order *simply* for partisan political advantage. He intended the policy to be effected. The fact that the Executive order was implemented within a decade was due to support from the White House, as well as to a good committee, the cooperation of the military command, and (in the case of the Army) the accident of the Korean conflict.

One factor that a President must consider when he selects this means for action is that a formal order may be disobeyed, in which case he will lose prestige. As Richard E. Neustadt has pointed out, in the last analysis, Presidential power is the power to persuade, not command.[73] In this instance, however, Truman knew that he was not restricted by overwhelming administrative opposition. The Executive order speeded up a process already under way in the Navy, and beginning in the Air Force and Army.

The President must also consider the possibilities of reversal by the courts and of congressional reprisal. The former was not a risk in this case, as the President's independent constitutional authority over the armed forces has seldom been questioned. As to the latter, Congress had shown little inclination to either prohibit or permit segregation in the armed forces. Indeed, Congress later tacitly approved the Executive order by refusing to pass legislation that would have permitted segregated military units.

Chapter III

FAIR
EMPLOYMENT PRACTICES

On July 2, 1964, President Lyndon B. Johnson went before a nationwide television audience to sign a civil rights bill that had been approved by Congress and sent to his desk only hours earlier. Selected members of the House and Senate, several Cabinet officers, and leaders in the civil rights movement gathered at 6:45 P.M. in the largest room in the White House, the East Room, for the signing ceremony. Title VII of this bill, which was the most comprehensive civil rights measure to pass since Reconstruction, banned discriminatory employment practices and created a five-member Equal Employment Opportunity Commission with enforcement responsibilities. For those who had tried to get a fair employment practices bill through Congress, this marked the culmination of an effort that had spanned more than two decades.

During that interval, Presidents Roosevelt, Truman, Eisenhower, and Kennedy each pursued a goal of fair employment practices by using the Executive order.

It may help at the outset to briefly identify these policies and the machinery established to implement them. President Roosevelt declared a policy of nondiscrimination in the employment of any person in war industries or in government agencies concerned with vocational and training programs. He established a Committee on Fair Employment Practice (FEPC) to achieve the purposes of Executive Order No. 8802 (June 25, 1941). He later appointed a second Committee on Fair Employment Practice, with redefined powers and duties (Executive Order No. 9346, May 27, 1943). President Truman gave the FEPC the additional authority to investigate minority problems in reconverted industries (Executive Order No. 9664, December 18, 1945). Congress terminated the wartime FEPC by cutting off funds on June 30, 1946.

President Truman tried to revitalize the nondiscrimination clause in government contracts by establishing new enforcement machinery: a Committee on Government Contract Compliance (Executive Order No. 10308, December 3, 1951). He also required a policy of nondiscrimination in government employment and established in the Civil Service Commission a Fair Employment Board with coordinating and advisory responsibilities (Executive Order No. 9980, July 26, 1948).

President Eisenhower replaced the Committee on Government Contract Compliance with the Government Contract Committee (Executive Order No. 10479, August 13, 1953), and the Fair Employment Board with the Committee on Government Employment Policy (Executive Order No. 10590, January 18, 1955). He charged both committees to strengthen the programs for ensuring nondiscrimination in employment.

When Kennedy assumed the Presidency, he combined the functions of the two Eisenhower committees and created a Committee on Equal Employment Opportunity. He gave this group increased powers and responsibilities for implementing nondiscrimination policies in both government and private employment (Executive Order No. 10925, March 6, 1961). After the Civil Rights Act of 1964 banned discriminatory employment practices and created an Equal Employment Opportunity Commission, President Johnson abolished the Kennedy committee and transferred its functions to the Civil Service Commission and the Department of Labor (Executive Order No. 11246, September 24, 1965).

These actions differed from Truman's response to demands for military desegregation, discussed in the previous chapter, in one important respect. In the area of fair employment, most of the demands and recommendations made by civil rights supporters were for statutes. Hence, the burden of pressure upon the President was for legislative leadership rather than for independent executive action. Why, under these circumstances, did the President use the Executive order?

Existing National Policy and Practice

President Roosevelt and his successors did not have a *tabula rasa* on which they could write new policies of fair employment practices. They stepped into a stream of developing policy. Rather than innovation, the pattern of Presidential activity was one of incremental change —a reemphasis upon a mandate against discrimination and a search for adequate machinery to enforce this mandate.

Before Roosevelt issued Order 8802, congressional and administrative declarations of nondiscrimination policies already existed. The Civil Service Act of 1883 committed the executive branch to make civil service appointments on the basis of merit and fitness, even though the Civil Service Commission did not interpret this as requiring the enforcement of nondiscrimination.[1] In November of 1940, however, new civil service rules did specifically prohibit racial discrimination. That same year, when Congress renovated the civil service system, it included a nondiscrimination clause in the Classification Extension Act of 1940. This was not given wide application, as the White House interpreted the clause as applying only to the classification of employees and not to their actual hiring or firing.[2]

Despite these and other declarations of nondiscriminatory employment policies, no supporting administrative machinery or sanctions for enforcement existed prior to World War II. With the war, increased manpower needs prompted scattered protests against discriminatory employment practices in the national defense industries.

Advantages of Legislation

Because of the ineffectiveness of existing law, further governmental action was needed if the objective of fair employment was to be reached. Especially in the field of private employment, congressional action was clearly advantageous. The President has ample constitutional authority as Chief Administrator to prohibit discrimination in employment within the executive branch. But with regard to private employment, the argument for Presidential action is based solely upon the implied duty of the President, under his oath of office to uphold a Constitution that affirms equal rights, to see that federal money is not used to support discriminatory practices. The means found for accomplishing this is to include provisions in government contracts that will eliminate discrimination in work done for the government.

The fact that Congress refused to pass fair employment practices legislation until 1964 has raised the question of the propriety of Presidential action, under implied constitutional authority, to enforce policies that Congress has failed to approve. This fundamental point was at issue when President Truman directed the Secretary of Commerce by

Executive order to seize the nation's steel mills. The Supreme Court declared the President's action unconstitutional. The crucial point of the opinion was that inasmuch as Congress could have ordered the seizure of the steel mills, the President had no power to do so without congressional authorization.

Sharing this view, Senator J. William Fulbright, Democrat of Arkansas, told reporters after President Truman established the Government Contract Compliance Committee that he did not think it was "a proper practice" for the executive branch to attempt to put into effect, through contracts, measures that Congress had refused to approve.[3] On the other hand, those who argue that Congress's failure to pass fair employment practices legislation does not prevent the President from entering that field can point to the fact that in many instances both President and Congress have acted at different times on the same subjects.[4] None of the Presidents' actions considered in this chapter were challenged in the courts.

Executive action taken under Presidential prerogative has certain limitations that legislation does not. Financing is one handicap. Insufficient funds made it impossible for the committees created by Executive orders to establish regional offices where they were badly needed, except in the case of Roosevelt's second FEPC. Likewise, the committees could not hire an adequate staff of investigators and attorneys.

Rather than seek specific congressional appropriations for unauthorized committees, and thereby subject them to a possible kiss of death on Capitol Hill, Presidents for years resorted to the "Special Projects" or "Emergency Fund" in the Executive Office appropriation. Clearly with Roosevelt's FEPC in mind, Congress attacked the Presidential practice of establishing committees and funding them in this way. The 1944 Russell Amendment to the Independent Offices Appropriation Act of 1940 prohibited the use of funds to pay expenses of any agency (including those established by Executive order) that had been in existence for more than one year without a specific appropriation. After passing the Russell Amendment, Congress twice appropriated money for the FEPC. The second time, in 1946, was for liquidating the Committee's affairs.

In the Independent Offices Appropriation Act of 1946, Congress became more permissive and authorized the participating executive departments to pay the expenses of interdepartmental committees engaged in activities of common interest to the departments. All the Presidential committees considered in this chapter were interdepartmental committees, with the exception of Roosevelt's FEPC and the Fair Employment Board, the latter of which was funded and staffed by the Civil Service Commission.

A statutory commission, it should be noted, is not necessarily assured of adequate financing. It is entirely possible that departments might contribute more for the activities of an interdepartmental committee than would be forthcoming if a statutory commission were involved in appropriations battles on the Hill.

Coverage is another obstacle for executive programs. Presidential staffs found no way to regulate the employment practices of private enterprise, other than through the device of the government contract. Therefore, a fair employment practices Executive order cannot directly reach thousands of firms that are not parties to government contracts. Similarly, the President has claimed no legal power over labor unions, and since unions are not parties to government contracts, he cannot reach them by Executive order except, perhaps, through hearings and publicity.

Many of the cases of unfair practices that were referred to the committees had to be closed for lack of jurisdiction. Approximately 36 percent of the complaints received by President Eisenhower's Government Contract Committee, for example, were not within the scope of the Executive order.[5] Nevertheless, the coverage under Executive orders was significant, involving over 2½ million civilian employees in the national government, and 20 million or more employed by government contractors. This makes the government contract a most powerful instrument for accomplishing nondiscrimination objectives.

Another limitation on the committees established by Executive order is that they have no power to intervene directly in situations of unfair employment practices. They cannot resort to court enforcement, as does a statutory commission that is enforcing a penal law. Nevertheless, the lack of strong enforcement powers was generally not considered to be a severe restriction. The members found that conciliation and persuasion were the most effective tools in promoting equal economic opportunity in American business and industry. Indeed, when the statutory Equal Employment Opportunity Commission was finally established, its first chairman, Franklin D. Roosevelt, Jr., announced that the accent would be on conciliation and persuasion.[6] If Presidential power is the power to persuade, in large measure this is also true of governmental power in general in the field of social change.

Pressures for New Policies

Because of the greater potential effectiveness of legislation, most of the pressure for fair employment policies focused on congressional action. Most unions—particularly the Congress of Industrial Organizations—began demanding a strong federal antidiscrimination program toward the end of World War II. By 1949 the National Association for the Advancement of Colored People had declared an FEPC law to be the "the No. 1 objective" in the civil rights program. The National

Urban League had given top priority to the question of equal employment opportunities since its organization in 1910. Continued pressure was also exerted by the National Council for a Permanent FEPC, organized in 1943 by A. Philip Randolph and others for the sole purpose of securing a fair employment practices statute with enforcement powers. Although originally a New York group, the Council grew to include almost seventy cooperating national organizations, including church, labor, civil libertarian, Negro, Jewish, fraternal, and professional groups.

In addition, many other groups met in Washington at different times to urge support for FEPC legislation. These included the 1950 National Emergency Civil Rights Mobilization, sponsored by fifty-five organizations; the 1952 Leadership Conference on Civil Rights, with delegates from fifty member organizations; and the March on Washington for Jobs and Freedom, organized by A. Philip Randolph in 1963.

The Presidents of the United States were pledged to support fair employment practices legislation because of promises made in the party platforms, beginning with the 1944 Republican platform and the 1948 Democratic platform. Furthermore, various Presidential committees advised the Chief Executives to seek FEPC legislation. These included Roosevelt's Committee on Fair Employment Practice, Truman's Committee on Civil Rights, and Eisenhower's Government Contract Committee.

Within the executive branch itself, the Department of Labor consistently advocated legislation to prohibit discrimination in private employment. On one occasion Eisenhower's Labor Secretary, James P. Mitchell, who was also vice-chairman of the Government Contract Committee, even openly supported compulsory fair employment practices legislation contrary to administration policy. Similarly, Secretary of Labor Arthur J. Goldberg endorsed an FEPC bill "in principle" prior to President Kennedy's support of legislation.

Despite this widespread advocacy of fair employment practices legislation, a coordinated campaign in opposition never developed. Opponents obviously felt they could depend upon anti-civil-rights congressmen to stop its enactment. Few testified at congressional hearings against proposed FEPC bills. In fact, at some of the hearings no hostile witnesses appeared. What active opposition there was to the FEPC movement came mostly from organizations representing businessmen, such as the National Association of State Chambers of Commerce, the United States Wholesale Grocers' Association, and the Southern States Industrial Council, an organization of Southern manufacturers.

Congressional Action

In spite of the wide support for fair employment legislation, a brief survey of congressional action before 1964, when the Civil Rights Act passed, shows that FEPC supporters were unable to get a law past procedural barriers. During this time no FEPC bill even came to a vote in the Senate, and on only one occasion did such a bill pass in the House. The bills proposed were of two general types: those with enforcement or penalty provisions (compulsory), and those with persuasive or educational provisions (voluntary).

The first FEPC bill was introduced in the House by Vito Marcantonio, American Labor Party of New York, in 1942, during President Roosevelt's third term in office. Although Roosevelt had stated during his 1940 campaign that he believed Congress should pass a law making the Committee on Fair Employment Practice permanent, fair employment practices never became part of his legislative program. Truman was the first President to seek fair employment legislation, and he did so throughout most of his administration. In 1945 he gained a moment of glory among civil rights proponents when he sent a letter to the chairman of the Rules Committee calling for a rule to permit a bill establishing a permanent FEPC to reach the floor. Truman's effort was well-publicized, and gained support for the President among civil rights proponents,[7] but it failed.

In the Senate, the Committee on Education and Labor favorably reported an FEPC bill in 1945 during the 79th Congress. When it finally reached the floor, it ran into a complicated filibuster, and after cloture failed the measure was not revived.

In the 80th Congress, the Education and Labor Committee took no action on fifteen FEPC bills introduced in the House. However, the Senate Committee on Labor and Public Welfare favorably reported a bipartisan FEPC bill in February, 1948. The Majority Policy Committee scheduled the measure for floor action in April. But the Republican leaders, pessimistic about its chances and afraid that any attempt to bring the bill to the floor would result in a Southern filibuster, never called it up.

The closest that supporters of FEPC legislation came to success during the Truman administration was in the 81st Congress. In April, 1949, administration-sponsored FEPC bills were introduced in the House and Senate. The House Education and Labor Committee reported the bill, but the Rules Committee again declined to clear it. Then early in 1950 the chairman of the Education and Labor Committee took the bill away from the Rules Committee under the "21-day rule" and sent it to the floor. After lengthy debate, a voluntary FEPC bill was substituted for the original compulsory plan, and the amended bill passed the House 240 to 177. This was to be the only time that a fair employment practices bill passed either house. In the Senate the Committee on Labor and Public Welfare reported the companion bill without recommendation. But a filibuster blocked decision on a motion to take up the measure, and after cloture attempts failed twice, proponents allowed the bill to die. Following the 1950 defeat, President Truman made no further major effort to secure civil rights legislation.

The incoming Eisenhower administration showed little interest in seeking FEPC legislation. Dozens of bills were introduced in every session but died in committee. The House took no action during Eisenhower's administration. In the Senate the Labor and Public Welfare Committee conducted hearings and favorably reported a bipartisan bill in 1954, but it never reached the floor.

On one occasion during his second term, President Eisenhower did include a provision for a statutory Commission on Equal Job Opportunity under Government Contracts in the administration's omnibus civil rights bill. After the House Judiciary Committee deleted it, Chairman Emanuel Celler said that an "unholy alliance" of Southern Democrats and Republicans was responsible for its removal.[8] The chair ruled out of order attempts to restore the provision on the House floor.

When the Senate Judiciary Committee conducted hearings on the House-passed omnibus bill, New York Republican Kenneth B. Keating offered the fair employment practices provision as a Committee amendment, but this move failed. In one more attempt, his fellow New York Republican, Jacob Javits, offered the deleted provision on the Senate floor. Minority leader Everett Dirksen, Senate sponsor of the administration bill, undercut the effort by moving to table the amendment, and the motion carried 48 to 38. Dirksen explained that he did not want the provision to "jeopardize passage" of a civil rights bill, and that he had requested the President not to include it in the original administration measure.[9] Subsequently the bill did pass, and the President signed the Civil Rights Act on May 6, 1960.

When John F. Kennedy entered the White House, he refused to support fair employment legislation until the 88th Congress. In 1963 members of both political parties introduced a number of broad civil rights bills, including an administration-sponsored ommibus bill. After conducting extensive hearings, a subcommittee of the House Judiciary Committee reported an omnibus civil rights bill that included a section creating a Federal Equal Employment Opportunity Commission. Minority party members of the subcommittee charged that previously prepared amendments were forced through by the Democratic majority. The bipartisan harmony on the subject disappeared, they asserted, the day the tax reduction bill, which needed their support, was finally passed.[10]

After several days of intense negotiations among administration spokesmen, Northern Democrats and Republicans on the Judiciary Committee, and the House leadership of both parties, the full Judiciary Committee reported a bipartisan civil rights bill. It contained less sweeping provisions than those reported by the subcommittee, but even so it was broader than the original administration measure. The major worry about the future of the new bipartisan bill was the reported resentment of many conservative Republicans over the Equal Employment Opportunity Commission provision. However, the 88th Congress finally did pass the bill with this provision, and President Johnson signed the Civil Rights Act of 1964 on July 2.

Pages of congressional testimony, debate, and dialogue had accumulated during the two decades in which supporters of fair employment legislation attempted to get a bill through Congress. During this time the House Rules Committee had never approved an FEPC bill for floor debate and a vote, and no FEPC bill had ever come to an actual vote in the Senate. Now at last a fair employment practices provision attached to an omnibus civil rights bill had passed. The Civil Rights Act of 1964, in effect, gave congressional endorsement to the policies established by the Presidential orders that are the subject of the following pages.

Presidential Action

Proponents of FEPC legislation argued that the function of implementing nondiscrimination policies in government and in private employment under government contract should not be subject to revocation or modification by successive Presidents. In practice, however, this type of modification has turned out to be precisely the advantage. The history of the protracted effort to discover an adequate method for enforcing fair employment policies reveals that this device permits experimentation in finding solutions to complex policy problems. The flexibility of policy-making by Executive order enables the President to revise policy and to devise enforcement machinery as rapidly as political circumstances permit.

President Roosevelt did not seek fair employment practices legislation, but responded to pressures for an Executive order by issuing one. From the beginning of his administration President Truman sought FEPC legislation and used the Executive order when he could not get congressional action. Both Eisenhower and Kennedy relied initially upon the Executive-order programs rather than pushing for legislation. Only later in their terms did they support fair employment bills. President Johnson's emphasis was upon legislative leadership. Our concern is the factors that prompted these strategies.

President Roosevelt did not have a civil rights program and never made specific civil rights proposals in his State of the Union messages. However, in his eleventh annual message, delivered on January 11, 1944, he asked Congress to help implement an "Economic Bill of

Rights" under which "a new basis of security and prosperity can be established for all—regardless of station, race, or creed." This reflects his emphasis upon helping Negroes by opening new economic opportunities for all Americans, rather than by planning specific programs for Negroes.

Malcolm Ross, who served as chairman of the second Committee on Fair Employment Practice, believed that Roosevelt was deeply concerned with full justice for Negroes.[11] Nevertheless, spokesmen for Negro groups had difficulty gaining access to the President. During the 1940 election campaign, the first Negro delegation to meet with Roosevelt in this period of mobilization for defense had a disappointing discussion on the utilization of Negro manpower by the armed forces.[12] After the 1940 conference, repeated attempts to see the President were met with rebuffs. Negro morale dropped as they saw themselves excluded from the jobs with adequate wages that opened in 1940 when the United States began the transition to a war economy. Before or after Pearl Harbor, few statements on the war by prominent Negro leaders failed to mention that for Negroes it was a war for democracy both abroad and at home.[13]

Negro protests became increasingly sharp. As described in Chapter II, A. Philip Randolph, President of the Brotherhood of Sleeping Car Porters, conceived the idea of a march on Washington in early 1941. A March-on-Washington Committee was formed and the march officially scheduled for July 1. At first the idea was coolly received among the predominantly conservative Negro leadership. But the credit for attempts by the administration to placate the Negroes, including antidiscrimination memoranda issued by the Office of Production Management and the White House, was given by Negro newspapers to the MOWC and added to the momentum of the movement.[14]

As the MOWC gained public attention through the mass media, the administration could no longer ignore the movement. Lester B. Granger, a member of the MOWC, wrote that the administration obviously did not want thousands of Negroes protesting in the capital "at a time when a semblance of unity was most essential to national prestige."[15] Mrs. Roosevelt argued in a letter to Randolph that the march might do more harm than good to the Negro cause, especially if an incident should occur that might "create in Congress even more solid opposition from certain groups than we have had in the past."[16] According to one report, "the treatment Negro demonstrators might receive from Southern-reared white Washingtonians, including the police, weighed heavily in Mrs. Roosevelt's objections to the March."[17]

On June 13 Mayor La Guardia of New York City, who was also head of the Office of Civilian Defense, together with Mrs. Roosevelt and Aubrey Williams, director of the National Youth Administration, met in the mayor's office with A. Philip Randolph and Walter White, executive secretary of the NAACP. The Negro representatives were promised that plans would be made to secure jobs for Negroes in national defense and were asked to call off the scheduled Washington demonstration.[18] Foreseeing more promises, rather than a concerted effort to meet their two demands of integration of the military and nondiscrimination in employment in defense industries, they refused.

Other attempts failing, on June 18 the President conferred with A. Philip Randolph, Frank R. Crosswaith, Layle Lane, and Walter White, and strongly urged them to cancel the march. The President said it was his intention to eliminate discrimination against Negroes in national defense and to use his office for accomplishing that task, but he was reluctant to issue the Executive order that was demanded.[19]

He did appoint a committee, with La Guardia as chairman, to confer with the members of the March-on-Washington Committee and draw up a plan to solve the problem. On June 24 La Guardia and Aubrey Williams, meeting with Randolph and three of his aides, presented a draft of an Executive order. After telephone conferences between Randolph and Walter White, and after the order was revised to include government agencies, Randolph approved the draft and called off the march.[20]

President Roosevelt issued Executive Order No. 8802 on June 25, 1941. The order stated a policy of nondiscrimination in the employment of workers in defense industries or government because of race, creed, color, or national origin. It directed departments and agencies concerned with vocational and training programs for defense production to take special measures to assure equal opportunity. It also directed contracting agencies to include a nondiscrimination clause in all defense contracts. The order established a Committee on Fair Employment Practice in the Office of Production Management to "receive and investigate complaints of discrimination in violation of the provisions of this order," to "take appropriate steps to redress grievances which it finds to be valid," and to recommend to federal agencies steps to carry out the terms of the order.

The Committee was subjected to constant sniping in Congress, and Roosevelt was never able to give it his full support. While he did not want to lose Northern votes, he feared that angering Southern conservatives unduly would result in lengthy filibusters harmful to the administration's program.

Roosevelt's dilemma is illustrated by the decision to transfer the Committee to the War Manpower Commission. Although the FEPC had been established in the Office of Production Management, it operated as an independent agency, funded from the President's emergency fund and responsible solely to the President. This arrangement had continued when the FEPC was moved on January 26, 1942, to the War Production Board after the OPM was abolished. But in June, 1942, the Committee went into the South for the first time and held hearings in Birmingham, Alabama. Upon his return from Birmingham, the chairman received White House congratulations for a job well done, and plans were approved by the White House for a broad nationwide offensive to enforce No. 8802.[21] At the height of their optimism, FEPC members were astonished on July 30 when the President, without consulting any of them, transferred the Committee to the War Manpower Commission.[22] There it would be under Paul V. McNutt's direct supervision and funded through regular budgetary channels. This move was apparently made to restrict the Committee's activities. As the Washington bureau of the NAACP pointed out, the transfer gave Southern congressmen the opportunity to limit or eliminate funds for FEPC.[23] Roosevelt's action was probably the result of heavy pressure which congressmen and other political leaders in Southern states put on him following the Alabama hearings. One writer believes that other groups were also behind the transfer: Northern industrial interests, "lily-white" trade unions, and top government officials who had been annoyed by FEPC efforts to end discrimination in their departments and agencies.[24]

One of the principal concerns of the Negro leaders from the beginning had been that the FEPC remain an independent agency responsible only to the President. They believed the President to be more susceptible to their demands than Congress or administrative officials.[25] In response to the rising public clamor from minority, liberal, labor, and religious groups over the transfer, President Roosevelt issued a statement on August 17 in which he defended his action and explained that it was his "intention to strengthen, not to submerge, the Committee" by making the resources and personnel of the WMC available to it. He said that it would have the "friendly supervision" and assistance of McNutt.[26] This was hardly the case. The underlying friction between McNutt and the FEPC finally exploded on January 11, 1943, when McNutt, without consulting the Committee, postponed the FEPC's scheduled hearings on complaints against twenty-three railroads, mainly in the South, and several unions. Shortly thereafter, the chairman of the FEPC and two members resigned, and the Committee's status became uncertain. Malcolm Ross reports that after Attorney General Francis Biddle and others in Washington became concerned over the FEPC's moribund condition, the President requested that McNutt and Biddle meet with representatives of minority-group organizations to discuss plans for revising and strengthening the Committee's scope and powers.[27]

The minority-group leaders demanded that the FEPC be removed from the jurisdiction of the War Manpower Commission and be restored to its former independent status.[28] The FEPC itself also urged that the Committee be returned to its independent status and adequately financed.[29] As a consequence Executive Order 9346, issued May 27, 1943, established a new Committee on Fair Employment Practice in the Office for Emergency Management of the Executive Office of the President. In addition to defense contracts covered in the old order, the new one required that a nondiscrimination clause be included in all contracts. The Committee was again authorized to "receive and investigate complaints of discrimination forbidden by the Order" and to "conduct hearings, make findings of fact, and take appropriate steps to obtain elimination of such discrimination."

Enemies of the nondiscrimination principle continued their opposition. Incident followed incident until the second FEPC was killed in a congressional appropriations battle, to which it was subjected because of the Russell Amendment. On the day of Roosevelt's death, his secretary had telephoned Representative Adolph J. Sabbath, chairman of the Rules Committee, conveying the President's request that he do everything in his power to bring about adoption of a rule which would enable voting on the FEPC appropriation.[30]

As soon as Truman assumed office in April, 1945, the issue of fair employment practices legislation was brought to his attention. Not only was the FEPC the subject of a congressional appropriations battle, but the bill to establish a statutory FEPC was held up in the House Rules Committee. When Congress passed the National War Agencies Appropriation Act of 1946, it provided for liquidating the Committee on Fair Employment Practice. With the Committee lost, President Truman sent a widely publicized letter on June 6, 1945, to the Rules Committee chairman asking him to permit the bill establishing a permanent FEPC to come to a vote on the House floor. This failing, three months later the President included a request for a permanent FEPC in the twenty-one-point legislative program for reconversion to a peacetime economy that he sent to Congress.

Under the National War Agencies Appropriation Act, the Committee on Fair Employment Practice was scheduled for dissolution in June, 1946. In December, 1945, the Committee requested the President to send a letter to all government agencies asking their cooperation in the national policy of nondiscrimination in government service. The Committee also urged him to issue an Executive order extending Committee activities to reconverted industries.[31] The President, advised that the FEPC members would resign if the order were not issued, complied with both requests.[32] Although the terminal appropriation had already been voted for the Committee, Truman issued Executive Order No. 9664 (December 18, 1945), in order to give the FEPC the additional authority to investigate minority problems in reconverted industries until the Committee's termination date of June 30, 1946. On the same day he wrote the heads of all executive departments and agencies, asking them to review their personnel policies and procedures and to assure him that they were in accord with national policy expressed in civil service rules and existing law.[33] During 1946 and early 1947, the President repeated his recommendations for fair employment legislation in a radio address, State of the Union message, and Economic Report to Congress. So at least initially, President Truman intended to seek compliance without special administrative machinery and to use less formal directives than the Executive order, while at the same time pressing for legislation.

On December 5, 1946, Truman created his advisory Committee on Civil Rights. The Committee's report, submitted the following year, outlined recommendations for legislation, including a Fair Employment Practices Act. It also suggested that the President issue a mandate against discrimination in government and create adequate machinery to enforce it. In his Civil Rights message of February 2, 1948, President Truman recommended that Congress create a Fair Employment Practices Commission with authority to prevent discrimination by employers and labor unions, trade and professional associations, and government agencies and employment bureaus. He announced also that he would "shortly issue an Executive Order containing a comprehensive restatement of the federal nondiscrimination policy, together with appropriate measures to ensure compliance."

The Civil Service Commission prepared a preliminary draft of the proposed Executive order, but Presidential assistant Philleo Nash called it too weak. He felt that it would incur as much wrath as a stronger order and yet would not gain any favor.[34] After talking with Walter White and others from the NAACP in early February, Nash urged the creation of a special unit in the Civil Service Commission to review decisions, make rules, and coordinate policies and procedures.[35] The final draft, prepared by the Justice Department, provided for a Fair Employment Board in the Civil Service Commission.

As discussed in the previous chapter, President Truman had committed his administration to civil rights action, but this order, like the military desegregation order, was timed for the campaign. And like its companion, the fair employment order caused little comment when it was issued on July 26, 1948. Most Southerners agreed with a spokesman for the Civil Service Commission who, according to a *Washington Post* report, said that antisegregation rules had been in force within the Civil Service for years and that "the new orders would have little effect." It is true that the Executive order did reaffirm existing policy, but it also established an implementing agency to add some sanctions to previous policy. The President at least seemed to be intent upon pursuing a more vigorous course to eliminate discrimination in government employment.

After the fair employment order was issued, Truman continued to seek a method for meeting the problem in private employment, as the nondiscrimination clause had become a dead letter in government contracts. Because of the Russell Amendment, he moved cautiously. Once again he supported proposals for fair employment practices legislation in his 1949 State of the Union and Budget messages. He also gave instructions for preparation of an Executive order similar to the wartime FEPC to be issued "as soon as possible."[36]

On January 17, 1950, the President received a delegation from the National Emergency Civil Rights Mobilization Committee. Stephen J. Spingarn had advised him that "since the likelihood of enactment of any consequential civil rights legislation in 1950 seems remote, it would appear to be particularly desirable that the President take advantage of appropriate opportunities during 1950 to demonstrate (as we know to be the case) that he means what he has said about civil rights legislation."[37]

In 1950 a proposed Executive order creating an FEPC with enforcement powers was sent to the Bureau of the Budget by the Department of Labor. For several months it was the subject of discussion between government agencies and minority group organizations.[38] The Labor Department believed that the Russell Amendment prohibited the creation of an FEPC similar to Roosevelt's.[39] Attorneys for the NAACP, however, argued that the Russell Amendment did not prevent the creation of an FEPC because Congress appropriated funds directly to the Committee during the last two years of its existence.[40] When the question of a forthcoming Executive order came up at a press conference, the President told reporters that he would act at the proper time within the framework of the statutes and his authority.

Following the outbreak of the Korean crisis and during the period from February until November, 1951, Truman issued, under authority of the First War Powers Act of 1941, six Executive orders directing various government agencies to include nondiscrimination clauses in their procurement contracts. These efforts to revitalize the nondiscrimination clause in government contracts finally culminated in Executive Order No. 10308 of December 3, 1951, also issued under statutory authority. The head of each contracting agency was charged with primary responsibility for obtaining compliance. The order also created an interagency Government Contract Compliance Committee to assess the existing program and recommend to the agencies methods for improving its effectiveness.

The Attorney General advised the President that the letters of appointment should refer to the section of the act under which the appointments were made and should say that the President deemed such appointments necessary in order to carry out the provisions of the Defense Production Act of 1950.[41] When he released the text of the Executive order on December 3, Truman issued a statement in which he carefully related his order to his war powers.

Executive Order No. 10308 is important to note because of the President's concern over authority. In all probability, the lack of controversy following this order encouraged President Eisenhower to take further steps, without statutory authority, to implement nondiscriminatory employment policies through the instrument of the government contract.

In his first State of the Union message in 1953, President Eisenhower committed his administration to the cause of civil rights. However, he did not propose legislation, and he endorsed fair employment measures only indirectly, by stressing his intention to fulfill the pledges of the Republican platform.

Eisenhower contended that his predecessors had wasted most of their efforts pushing for civil rights legislation that habitually met defeat. He decided to use the executive approach. He asserted that much could be done by executive power alone to see that the federal house was in order and to eliminate segregation in all installations where federal money was spent.[42]

A persistent theme in President Eisenhower's statements on civil rights was a preference for executive rather than legislative action, a preference for state and local rather than national action, and a preference for voluntary rather than compulsory action. He repeatedly emphasized that "there are certain things that are not best handled by punitive or compulsory Federal law" and that he would take action only where "Federal authority clearly extends."[43]

After the Republican victory in November, members of President Truman's Committee on Government Contract Compliance began resigning. The chairman resigned January 16, 1953, and after that the Committee had only a fitful existence. Sherman Adams, assistant to President Eisenhower, learned of the plight of the leaderless committee in early February and was told that it could not function until it was restaffed and reactivated by the White House.[44]

The problem, apparently a matter of low priority, dragged on while the President and his staff dealt with more urgent matters at the beginning of a new administration. The catalyst that activated interest were questions on the status of the Committee asked by newsmen in at least three press conferences. After the first inquiry on April 2, Sherman Adams began to work on the matter together with his assistant, Maxwell

W. Rabb, who had general responsibility for civil rights matters, and two other staff aides, Gabriel Hauge and Bernard M. Shanley. The Bureau of the Budget recommended thanking the remaining members of the Committee and relieving them of their duties. However, the White House staff decided that the best method would be to discontinue the inherited committee and create a new one with a new name.[45]

Eisenhower decided to reaffirm the government's nondiscriminatory employment policy and to strengthen the provisions for their implementation. Waiting until after Congress had adjourned, he issued Executive Order No. 10479 on August 13, 1953. He established a precedent by appointing Vice President Richard M. Nixon chairman of the new Government Contract Committee in order to give it maximum prestige and authority. Previous committees had found that discrimination in employment could be eliminated through persuasion, providing the authority of the persuader was recognized.

The head of each contracting agency retained primary responsibility for obtaining compliance. This was done because the agencies employed approximately five thousand contracting and compliance officers, whose duties included investigating complaints filed with the Committee, conducting reviews of the compliance of government contractors, and administering the Committee's educational programs.

The Committee, with only a small staff, had more definite operating functions than did the Truman committee. It was charged with assisting the contracting agencies to develop better compliance machinery, such as an orderly system for processing complaints. It also helped the contracting agencies organize a program of cooperation with public and private groups working in the field and an educational program on the necessity and desirability of the national policy.

Meeting with members of the Committee on August 19, the President emphasized that he wanted concrete accomplishments, not publicity.[46] This was in keeping with Eisenhower's low-keyed approach to civil rights: he chose to sacrifice politically advantageous publicity for administrative advantage. Even where accomplishments were made, the tendency of the White House was to play them down. Indeed, some men close to the President believed that the administration went too far in underplaying its accomplishments in this area.[47]

One of the first actions of the Government Contract Committee was to revise and strengthen the nondiscrimination clause mandatory in government contracts. Issued by President Eisenhower in Executive Order No. 10557, September 3, 1954, the new clause required contractors to post a notice acknowledging their agreement to provide employment without discrimination because of race, religion, color, or national origin. This requirement meant that for the first time every contracting officer had to assume active responsibility for the program, and every government contractor had to comply publicly. The clause also made it clear that the contractual obligation to bar discrimination applied not only to initial hiring, but also to upgrading, demotion, transfer, recruitment, and other aspects of employment.

During his first term in office, President Eisenhower also established his own committee to ensure nondiscrimination in government service. Again, this was a remedial policy to cope with a situation that he inherited from the previous administration. Between 1952 and 1955 the Fair Employment Board had continued to supervise the government's employment policy, with little attention from the White House. In fact, the decision to issue Executive Order No. 10590 in early 1955 was invoked in part by the desires to eliminate a committee composed of older members who were unacceptable to the NAACP, and to squelch publication of a report to the President on Treasury Department resistance to a Fair Employment Board recommendation.[48] The White House had been sitting on the report to keep from involving the President in a conflict between a Presidentially established agency and a department head. However, newsmen picked up the story and at an April 29, 1954, press conference asked Eisenhower about the complaint of discrimination in the Treasury. Eisenhower answered that he "couldn't be expected to know too much about it." Maxwell Rabb felt that the awkward situation could be cured by abolishing the old committee, but he and various government officials agreed that such a move would arouse severe and justified public criticism unless a new one was created.[49] This President Eisenhower did by Executive Order No. 10590, January 18, 1955. He issued no Presidential statement to accompany the order and made no mention of it the following day at his news conference.

As in the case of the Government Contract Committee, the President enhanced the status of the new enforcement machinery by making the Committee on Government Employment Policy responsible solely to the White House. However, like its predecessor, the Committee was only advisory to the heads of the executive agencies, both with regard to their operating policies and with respect to the review of individual complaints.

These executive actions were holding operations and not enthusiastic commitments, for perhaps one of the same reasons that Eisenhower did not seek civil rights legislation during his first term. He considered civil rights to be a social problem and one not amenable to legislative solutions. There were also two other reasons for not seeking legislation. First, he believed it unlikely that Congress would pass a civil rights bill. Vice President Nixon had advised him that no matter how big and important the issue, the Democrat-controlled Congress would not let a civil rights measure out of committee.[50] And second, he feared that pressure for civil rights legislation might jeopardize the administration's other legislative programs.[51]

Nevertheless, in his State of the Union message in 1956 the President recommended that a bipartisan commission created by Congress thoroughly examine voting charges. He also announced that other proposals would be added to the civil rights program during 1956. Attorney General Herbert Brownell prepared draft legislation, and the entire Cabinet participated in discussions on the proposed civil rights program.[52] While Brownell argued for the strong Justice Department proposals, some in the Cabinet and on the White House staff advised the President that he was asking for trouble from the Southern Democrats in Congress.[53] Owing to the rift in the Cabinet over civil rights, it was not until April 9, 1956, that the President's recommendations were sent to the Capitol, and they did not mention fair employment practices.

In 1959 a provision for a Commission on Equal Employment Opportunity under Government Contracts was included in the administration's omnibus civil rights bill, despite the advice of Senate Minority Leader Everett Dirksen.[54] Administration forces in Congress sacrificed this provision, even though it was limited in jurisdiction to that of the existing program, to secure passage of the Civil Rights Act of 1960.

Like Eisenhower, President John F. Kennedy believed that in the civil rights struggle "we are confronted primarily with a moral issue."[55] However, he had more confidence in legislation as an aid to alleviating the problem than did Eishenhower. After the nominating convention, Kennedy formed a team to work on civil rights problems, and during the campaign he pledged legislative and executive leadership in that area. In September, 1960, he asked Senator Joseph S. Clark of Pennsylvania and Representative Emanuel Celler of New York to draft legislation on the party's civil rights pledges, one of which was a statutory FEPC.[56]

Following his inauguration, however, civil rights recommendations were conspicuously omitted when President Kennedy presented his legislative program in a State of the Union message, a budget message, and various special messages. After Clark and Celler introduced their bills in May, White House Press Secretary Pierre Salinger announced that they were "not Administration-backed bills."[57]

Kennedy's shift was probably due to his need for the votes of Southern Democrats to put over higher-priority administration measures. When pressed for an explanation of his position on civil rights at a news conference March 8, 1961, he said he believed that there were a "good deal of things we can do now in administering laws previously passed by the Congress, particularly in the area of voting, and also by using the powers which the Constitution gives to the President through

Executive orders." He added, "When I feel that there is a necessity for a congressional action, with a chance of getting that congressional action, then I will recommend it to the Congress." After a White House meeting in May, 1961, Senate Majority Leader Mike Mansfield said: "We want to get the program outlined by the President through, and after that we will consider civil rights if necessary."[58]

Instead of sponsoring legislation, President Kennedy issued Executive Order No. 10925 on March 6, 1961, in his first major civil rights move. Fred Lazarus, who was a member of Eisenhower's Government Contract Committee, and Abe Fortas, Washington attorney, were instrumental in drafting the order. Following Eisenhower's precedent, Kennedy designated the Vice President of the United States, Lyndon Johnson, as chairman of a new Committee on Equal Employment Opportunity, which replaced both the Government Contract Committee and the Committee on Government Employment Policy. The Secretary of Labor was named vice chairman and given specific responsibility for supervising the implementation of equal employment policies. The advantage to this was that the Labor Department has regional offices all over the country.

Probably the most important difference from previous orders was that Kennedy's required positive action to further equal employment opportunities, rather than merely prohibiting discriminatory practice. The order stated that "it is the policy of the Executive Branch of the Government to encourage by positive measures equal opportunity for all qualified persons within the Government." Furthermore, the order contained a much more comprehensive nondiscrimination clause that required a government contractor to take "affirmative action" to make certain that applicants were employed and employees treated without discrimination.

Executive Order No. 10925 went beyond all previous orders in the demands it made on government contractors and the powers it gave to the Committee. The antidiscrimination clause to be included in government contracts was for the first time to be at least partly self-enforcing through regularly required compliance reports. The Committee itself was empowered to investigate the employment policies of any government contractor or subcontractor, or such an inquiry could be initiated by the appropriate contracting agency or through the Secretary of Labor.

Two sections of the order set forth "carrot and stick" provisions. The Committee was authorized to award certificates of merit to companies fulfilling the provisions of the order. The sanctions and penalties to ensure compliance included publicity, contract termination, and prosecution by the Justice Department for contract violation and for furnishing false information.

Not until two and one-half years after Kennedy issued Executive Order No. 10925 did he ask for a program of new laws to protect the rights of minorities. Even then, he made no specific requests in the area of employment rights. But at a press conference in May, 1963, the President confirmed reports that the administration was considering new civil rights legislation as a result of events in the South during the spring. On the night of June 11, 1963, after the confrontation with Governor Wallace over the admission of Negroes to the University of Alabama, Kennedy said in an address to the nation that "the events in Birmingham and elsewhere have so increased the cries for equality that no city or state or legislative body can prudently choose to ignore them."

The President submitted new and broadened civil rights proposals to Congress on June 19, 1963. In these he included a request to strengthen the President's Committee on Equal Employment Opportunity by giving it a permanent statutory basis. He also pledged renewed "support of pending Federal Fair Employment practices legislation, applicable to both employers and unions."

During June and early July Kennedy met with scores of business leaders, labor leaders, religious leaders, educators, lawyers, and representatives of women's organizations to urge support for his civil rights program. The proposed bill subsequently passed and was signed into law on July 2, 1964, by President Johnson. The Civil Rights Act of 1964 included a fair employment section, which had been endorsed but not submitted by Kennedy, who had doubted its chances for acceptance.

Also in his June 19 Civil Rights message, President Kennedy repeated his announcement of June 4 that he would issue an Executive order extending the authority of the Committee on Equal Employment Opportunity to include the construction of buildings and other facilities undertaken wholly or in part as a result of grant-in-aid programs. This was done by Executive Order No. 11114, issued June 22, 1963. Although many construction programs undertaken by state and local governments and private agencies participating in the federal grant-in-aid programs contained nondiscrimination requirements, practices and enforcement had not been uniform.

Five days after the assassination of President Kennedy, President Johnson addressed a joint session of Congress on November 27, 1963, and set the tone for the next few months of his administration by saying, "let us continue." He said that the first tasks were on the Hill and that "no memorial oration or eulogy could more eloquently honor President Kennedy's memory than the earliest possible passage of the civil rights bill for which he fought so long." A month later, in his first State of the Union message on January 8, 1964, he urged that "this session of Congress be known as the session which did more for civil rights than the last hundred sessions combined."

For a variety of reasons—including the national temper at the time, the legislative leadership and behind-the-scenes work of President Johnson, intensive and effective lobbying, the cohesiveness of the bipartisan coalition of Republicans and Northern Democrats, and the role played by Senate Minority Leader Everett Dirksen—Congress passed the most sweeping civil rights measure of the century in 1964. With the added responsibilities for the federal government under the new law, President Johnson announced on December 10, 1964, that he had asked Vice President Hubert Humphrey to assume the task of coordinating the government's many programs on civil rights, including those on fair employment. Two months later the President formalized this arrangement by creating the President's Council on Equal Opportunity, established under independent constitutional authority and funded as an interdepartmental committee with the Vice President as chairman (Executive Order No. 11197, February 5, 1965). The Council was to review and assist in coordinating the activities of all departments and agencies of the federal government that had responsibilities for eliminating discrimination and promoting equal opportunity.

Humphrey wrote a long memorandum to the President on September 24, 1965, after he had studied the activities of the various federal agencies involved in the field of civil rights.[59] He said that "the time has now come when operating functions can and should be performed by departments and agencies with clearly defined responsibility for the basic program, and that interagency committees and other interagency arrangements would now only diffuse responsibility." Humphrey, who had introduced the controversial civil rights plank into the 1948 Democratic platform and who had served as chairman of the President's Committee on Equal Employment Opportunity, was suggesting now that the time had passed when it was necessary to have special administrative machinery in order to ensure compliance with a national policy of nondiscrimination.

Humphrey advised the President to abolish the Committee on Equal Employment Opportunity. He recommended that the Civil Service Commission be given responsibility for enforcing nondiscrimination in federal employment and that the Department of Labor be assigned to oversee compliance by government contractors. He also recommended that the President terminate the Council on Equal Opportunity. "I am satisfied," Humphrey wrote, "that the working relationships between departments and agencies have advanced to the point where the formal organizational structure of the Council is no longer essential."

President Johnson, who often said that his three years as chairman of the Committee on Equal Employment Opportunity had been among the most rewarding he had spent in over thirty-two years of government service, concurred with the Vice President's recommendations. He abolished the Committee and reassigned the civil rights functions according to the Vice President's recommendations (Executive Order No. 11246, September 24, 1965), and he also abolished the Council (Executive Order No. 11247, September 24, 1965).

At the President's invitation, 2,500 Americans assembled in Washington on June 1 and 2, 1966, for the first national conference ever held on civil rights. The White House Conference "To Fulfill These Rights" concentrated on four areas: economic security and welfare, education, housing, and administration of justice. No recommendations were made that new policies on fair employment practices be established by Executive order. Clearly the time had passed when the President needed to act under his independent constitutional authority in this area.

Enforcement of Fair Employment Practices

The field of discriminatory employment practices is not one in which progress can be accurately defined, since the entire employment relationship is fraught with immeasurable subjective factors, such as the personality of an employee or the reasons for choices that appointing officials make from the top three names certified to them by the Civil Service Commission. All the Presidentially established fair employment practices committees obtained helpful statistical information on racial patterns in employment. But for several reasons, this information is of limited use as a yardstick of progress. Accurate statistical data for previous years are unavailable for comparative purposes. Furthermore, even if it is established that a racial pattern is present in an area of employment, this does not necessarily confirm either the existence or the absence of discrimination.

Moreover, if a precise statistical picture of discriminatory employment patterns could be devised, we still would not know with accuracy the extent to which employers, union leaders, and government executives changed their practices because of a certain Executive-order program or because of other factors. Consequently, conclusions with regard to the effectiveness of the fair employment Executive orders are impressionistic. It may also be noted that a comprehensive examination of the enforcement of a policy over almost two decades would take many more pages than necessary for the purpose of this book. The main point to be made here in order to demonstrate the significance of policymaking by Executive order is that these declarations of policy were applied with some effect.

The records of the various committees are a mixture of success and failure, as is true in the implementation of most policies. Much depended upon the committee members, the cooperation of the agency heads, and the support of the President. Of course, in the last analysis, as in the administration of other programs, the ultimate effectiveness depended upon the cooperation of thousands of administrators not only in Washington but in the field, where about 90 percent of all government employees are located. The Government Contract Committee, for example, learned after its new regional office was established in Chicago that its directives and instructions were not being received by the staff in the field and that where they were received, they were not getting serious attention.[60]

The story of the effort of seven committees to enforce a nondiscrimination policy is the story of a program that began experimentally and cautiously and gradually developed momentum, owing to increasing experience and stronger mandates in succeeding Executive orders. President Roosevelt's Committee on Fair Employment Practice pioneered methods for enforcing government policy in a controversial field. Inadequately funded, the first FEPC (June 25, 1941—May 27, 1943) had only a small staff in Washington and was forced to handle by correspondence most of the complaints that it received. Nevertheless, the Committee did devise policies for acting on complaints. It also decided upon the public hearing as a device for publicizing its work and for bringing pressure on companies through open disclosure of discriminatory practices. Significantly, the committee found that the war industries involved in hearings showed a higher utilization of minority group workers than those which did not participate in hearings.[61]

The second FEPC (May 27, 1943—June 28, 1946) had the benefit of a full-time chairman and more adequate financing. Consequently it was able to expand operations to fifteen field offices, and it gained experience in devising rules for field procedures to determine bona fide complaints and to make informal investigations. It also established procedures for the Committee to weigh complaints not adjustable in the field and to conduct public hearings in difficult cases.

The FEPC reported that during the five years, the two Roosevelt committees "satisfactorily settled" nearly 5,000 cases by peaceful negotiation. Although the bulk of the work was accomplished by quiet persuasion, on occasion the FEPC issued "directives." However, these were a "rigorous method of persuasion and not an act of compulsion," since the Committee had no enforcement powers. If persuasion failed, the FEPC called the parties to a public hearing. In a period of four years the Committee held thirty hearings involving 102 companies, 38 unions, and 5 government agencies.[62] The last recourse for the FEPC was to report a noncomplying company to the President, but this was resorted to only twice. One instance was a controversial case against 23 railroads and 14 labor unions. The Committee considered this to be one of its outstanding failures. After 14 Southern railroads denied that the Committee had jurisdiction, the case was reported to the President, who appointed a special committee to represent him in dealing with the issues. Malcolm Ross, the last chairman of the FEPC, was largely responsible for this move, and he later considered it to be "an irretrievable mistake," as there was never a showdown and the railroad cases quietly died over a period of two years.[63]

Another instance involved the Philadelphia Transportation Company and what was first an unaffiliated union and later the Transport Workers Union of America, CIO. This case dragged on for two years, and finally an actual attempt to hire Negroes as operators was made in July, 1944, following a War Manpower Commission requirement that the company hire without regard to race. The white operators went out on strike; the President then seized the properties, the Army operated them, the Negro motormen remained, and with the hiring barrier broken, no further incident resulted.

Since about 25 percent of the FEPC's case load came from government sources, the Committee also developed special procedures to handle problems of discrimination in government employment. In order to avoid duplication, the Committee arranged with several departments and agencies that the operating agency would exhaust its own remedies in eliminating discrimination, that it would inform the FEPC about the handling of its own cases, and that the FEPC would enter the case when it appeared insoluble by the agency.

After the Committee's demise in 1946, nondiscrimination policies in employment continued to be governed by a few statutory provisions, civil service regulations, some departmental and agency rules, and the policy declared in President Roosevelt's Executive orders. However, it became obvious that special machinery was necessary to prod government and private employers. The wartime gains of Negro, Mexican-American, and Jewish workers, the FEPC observed in its *Final Report* in 1946, were being lost "through an unchecked revival of discriminatory practices."

The problems created by reconversion to a peacetime economy aggravated the usual employment handicaps of the Negro in both government and private employment. His wartime gains had been in war industries, temporary war agencies, and the Army Service Forces and Naval shore establishments, all of which were rapidly demobilizing. Although statistics to show the extent of discrimination are unavailable, witnesses before congressional committees in the late forties testified that not only was discrimination in government, as well as in business and labor unions, widespread, but it had increased sharply since the end of World War II.[64]

President Truman's Fair Employment Board built on the FEPC's experience in establishing procedures for the correction of injustices brought to light through the complaint process. The Board learned, however, that the number of formal complaints, which had been anticipated as the main thrust of the attempt to secure nondiscriminatory employment practices, could not be accepted as a true index of discrimination in government.[65] Therefore the Board began experimenting with a positive corrective program in cooperation with the departments and agencies, and subsequent committees also emphasized this function.

The Board was successful not only in laying the groundwork for advances in the implementing machinery, but also in making administrators aware of the need to see that eligible men were treated fairly. The labor secretary of the NAACP and Presidential assistant David K. Niles, for example, were pleased with the effectiveness of the Board in several instances with which they had contact.[66] In fact, one respected member of the Board resigned in the spring of 1952 because he felt that the initial inertia had been overcome and the task ahead was just to keep the program moving.[67] By that time, one-third of the government agencies had hired Negroes as supervisors of mixed white and Negro groups or had employed them as executives and top-level scientific and professional workers for the first time in their history.[68] Part of this success can be attributed to the support of the President, as well as to occasional White House prodding of uncooperative agencies.[69]

President Eisenhower did not seem to attach the importance to the work of the Board that Truman did. And when he did establish its successor, the new Committee on Government Employment Policy got off to a slow start. The selection of an executive director bogged down in disagreements over approach.[70] Nevertheless, the Committee did keep the program going, and built on the work of the Fair Employment Board. For example, one of the Board's handicaps had been the lack of factual knowledge concerning the extent to which minority groups were being employed in government. A study of Negro employment was repeatedly postponed during the Truman administration for fear of political repercussions.[71] To meet this need for current information, Eisenhower's Committee, despite the opposition of representatives of some of the larger agencies, conducted a survey in late 1955 in five large cities.

As a result of the study, the questions that the Committee focused on were why Negroes were not in higher-level jobs and whether qualified Negroes could advance to such jobs. Work on these questions went forward by means of consultations, training courses, and area conferences.[72] The Committee attempted to move cautiously in order to gain the respect and confidence of the agencies and departments, and to hold its conferences in various parts of the country without arousing criticism or resentment.[73]

Four years later, the Committee conducted a second survey of the same five cities and found an increase in the number of Negroes moving to better-paying and more responsible positions. However, the U.S. Civil Rights Commission contended that this did not necessarily indicate the effectiveness of the government's nondiscrimination program, as similar improvements occurred simultaneously in private enterprise.[74]

Eisenhower's other committee, the Government Contract Committee, can be credited with much of the spadework on employment practices in private enterprise, since the Truman Committee on Government Contract Compliance, during its one-year existence, functioned largely as a study group. The Eisenhower Committee established the machinery necessary for implementation of the nondiscrimination provision and made some progress in promoting the program among the leaders responsible for carrying it out. The Committee also concentrated on the problems of motivating and training minority-group youth, since a dearth of qualified Negro applicants often exists when new employment opportunities are opened to them. The U.S. Commission on Civil Rights concluded that this may have been the Committee's most significant contribution.[75]

Nevertheless, there were weaknesses in the effort. Even though the Vice President was chairman, stronger White House support and prodding might have helped in instances of uncooperative agencies. Nixon's request that agencies pursue a firmer compliance policy by denying contracts to companies with discriminatory records was largely ignored. Also, some evidence in the Eisenhower papers points to dissension within the Committee, and this may have reduced its effectiveness.[76]

President Kennedy took advantage of the experience gained under other Chief Executives when he replaced the Committee on Government Employment and the Government Contract Committee with his own Committee on Equal Employment Opportunity. Consolidating the functions that had formerly somewhat overlapped corrected at least one of the weaknesses of the previous programs.

The two previous groups had recognized the necessity for a program of positive action and an adequate body of objective, comparative information on the employment status of minority group members in government. Both of these were met with specific requirements in Executive Order No. 10925. For the first time, an Executive order instructed agencies and departments to take affirmative action to eliminate employment discrimination. It also directed the Committee to make an immediate study of government employment practices, and in response, the Committee decided to take an annual government-wide

census of minority employment. This not only made it possible to moni-
tor and appraise agency employment practices and establish a base for
corrective action, but also served as a tool for increasing the motivation
of agency management to take positive action.[77]

The first survey, conducted in June, 1961, bore out the contention
that most Negro employees were concentrated in the lower grades of
government employment and that relatively few had progressed to the
middle and upper ranks. Consequently, Vice President Johnson, whom
Kennedy had appointed chairman, instructed all agencies to make an
intensive survey of their personnel to seek out persons who had been
"passed over" unfairly because of their race, creed, color, or national
origin, and to adjust such situations.[78] Furthermore, Negro high school
and college graduates were intensively sought out and recruited for
government employment,[79] even though this step aroused congressional opposition. The second and third annual surveys showed a significant improvement in the employment status of Negroes.

Other changes prompted by the experiences of the preceding committee resulted in an improvement in the compliance program. In 1957
Eisenhower's Committee had attempted to review a contractor's employment practices in the absence of a complaint by instituting compliance surveys. A survey consisted of a physical inspection of the facility
by a compliance official of the contracting agency. Since this was slow,
as only approximately five hundred plants could be surveyed each year,
in 1959 the Eisenhower Committee began requesting annual reports
from the agencies. The Kennedy order made it a requirement that each
contractor submit an annual manpower profile as proof of affirmative
action.

In spite of the emphasis on positive action, the Committee on Equal
Employment Opportunity did not neglect the complaint procedure that
had been a basic ingredient of the government's nondiscrimination
program. All the committees recognized the complaint process as useful
in providing a method whereby the citizen might bring to the attention
of top officials any evidence of contractors not complying with the
program. The Equal Employment Opportunity Committee processed
an unprecedented number of complaints, a development attributed to
confidence on the part of employees that something would be done
about discriminatory situations.[80]

Also, the previous committees had occasionally been faced with an
uncooperative contracting agency. The new order gave the Committee
itself the authority to investigate complaints and to take final action,
including the imposition of sanctions. The emphasis was not upon sanctions, however, since one of the important aspects of the Committee's
work was the voluntary program. The Committee decided that public
expression of new purpose by employers and unions was an effective

stimulant to voluntary progress toward real equality of opportunity. Consequently, two programs to secure the voluntary cooperation of employers and unions in promoting equal employment opportunity were undertaken—Plans for Progress and Programs for Fair Practices. By 1963, 115 companies, employing more than five and one-half million persons, had signed Plans for Progress. These firms, some of which did not hold government contracts, agreed to take the initiative in removing discrimination in employment.[81] Data available indicate that almost 25 percent of the new employees of these companies were minority group members, including significant numbers in classifications from which they had previously been almost entirely excluded.[82]

The Committee was authorized to use its best efforts and all available publicity to induce labor unions to comply with the order. The Committee signed Programs for Fair Practices with 117 AFL-CIO international union affiliates that had a combined membership of almost thirteen million workers, representing about 85 percent of the AFL-CIO.[83] Programs for Fair Practices enlisted the active support of international union officials in the Committee's efforts to end employment discrimination. These voluntary programs illustrate the ability of a committee, established by Executive order, to overcome the limitations of legal power by utilizing Presidential prestige in attempting to solve a national problem.

One of the Committee's strengths was that it had active support from the Chief Executive. President Kennedy, and later President Johnson, participated in White House ceremonies at which Plans for Progress and Union Programs for Fair Practices were signed. The statements made on these occasions gave the work of the Committee and the cooperating groups good press coverage and demonstrated Presidential support. President Kennedy reinforced the Executive order policy in other ways. To be assured of progress, in 1963 he requested a company-by-company, plant-by-plant, union-by-union report from the Committee. On June 4, 1963, the President directed the Secretary of Labor to require that the admission of young workers to apprenticeship programs be on a completely nondiscriminatory basis. He also asked that all federal construction programs be reviewed to prevent any racial discrimination in hiring practice, either directly by the rejection of available qualified Negro workers or indirectly by the exclusion of Negro applicants for apprenticeship training.[84]

Labor leaders credited the Committee's success in securing changes both to its vigorous support by the President and to the assurance from Committee members that sanctions would be applied.[85] The President's Committee on Equal Employment Opportunity reported in 1963, for the first time, that "there has been a basic *change in attitude* on the part of most of the managers of American industry and the heads of our responsible labor unions."[86] This was substantiated at a Senate committee hearing in 1963 by witnesses who stated that they had been aware of a new attitude within the past year and felt it was due to the fact that Washington had been pressing harder.[87]

The efforts of the five Presidents did not eliminate discriminatory practices in private employment. The House Committee on Education and Labor concluded in 1963, after hearing twenty-eight witnesses over ten days, that "discrimination in employment because of race, religion, color, national origin, or ancestry is a pervasive practice" with an adverse effect upon the nation. Nevertheless, Executive leadership during two decades had some impact upon the employment opportunities of minority groups—enough, at any rate, for these groups themselves to appreciate the governmental efforts. For example, the executive director of the Chicago Urban League noted in 1961 that "the vast rise that we have made in the last 20 years came about largely because of the leadership that we did get from the government."[88] In 1966, the White House Conference "To Fulfill These Rights" endorsed the recommendation that state and local governments emulate the program of contract compliance under Executive Order No. 11246.

Furthermore, aside from the important positive achievements the Presidential committees may have made in opening jobs and avenues of promotion to members of minority groups, the President at least laid the groundwork for subsequent legislation and for statutory committees. When the Equal Employment Opportunity Commission was created by Congress in 1964, and when the Department of Labor and the Civil Service Commission assumed the responsibilities of the Committee on Equal Employment Opportunity in 1965, all benefited from the many studies made in previous years and from the pool of experienced personnel that had been developed.

Conclusion

From the case of the movement for fair employment practices, it is apparent that when widespread demand for legislation persists, the President may use the Executive order as an alternative to seeking congressional action. He may decide on this course in circumstances where he determines that the legislation is unlikely to pass or where he fears that he might jeopardize competing legislative priorities. At the outset of their administrations Presidents Truman, Eisenhower, Kennedy, and Johnson each pledged action in the field of civil rights, and, with the exception of Eisenhower, in the specific area of fair employment practices. The remaining decisions, therefore, were largely matters of alternatives and timing.

Since the President is able to influence employment practices in private industry only through the government contract, legislation was preferable to the Executive order. This was true from the standpoint of coverage, funds, and to some extent, enforcement. The decision to request legislation, however, hinged upon the intensity of demand for it in various years, Presidential estimates of the chances for success, and his appraisal of its likely effects upon his entire legislative program. An additional consideration in President Eisenhower's case was his lack of confidence in the legislative approach to civil rights problems.

When Roosevelt was President, there was little pressure for fair employment practices legislation. President Truman did seek such legislation at first, but dropped his proposals after repeated failures. Neither Eisenhower nor Kennedy initially sponsored a fair employment bill; it was clear to them that Congress was not inclined to pass one. Beginning in 1942, Congressmen opposing FEPC legislation had effectively used institutional procedures to block bills. Johnson successfully pushed for a statutory fair employment practices provision immediately after assuming the Presidency.

Roosevelt issued his Executive orders in response to demands for the orders. Truman issued an Executive order when he could not get congressional action, and timed its release to provide the Democrats with campaign material in 1948. Eisenhower was to some extent forced to issue his orders, because he had inherited Presidential committees from his predecessors. However, he timed neither of his for partisan political advantage. In fact, he made a point of trying to act quietly on this, as well as on other civil rights matters, for the purpose of avoiding controversy. President Kennedy issued his Executive order as an alternative to honoring a campaign commitment to press for civil rights legislation. Each established policies that were demanded by an articulate segment of the national constituency, but that were stymied in Congress.

While there was insufficient support for fair employment legislation to overcome inertia and procedural obstacles in both houses of Congress, there was also insufficient congressional opposition to discourage the President from acting. Furthermore, despite refusal to enact legislation, Congress tacitly approved the Presidential actions by failing to pass legislation reversing them. Congress might have attached riders, for example, to the appropriations bills that provided funds for the agencies participating in the interdepartmental committees.

A definite advantage of the Executive order as an instrument for policy-making can be seen in the history of the application of the non-discrimination policies. Roosevelt's successors continued to make adjustments and changes in emphasis in the federal government's nondiscrimination program by issuing superseding Executive orders. The Executive order method clearly permits flexibility in the attempt to find ways for coping with serious national social problems—in this instance, discriminatory employment practices. With so many complex national policy issues confronting the nation today, the Executive order could provide the instrument for experiment that is lacking within the relatively permanent molds of statutory law. In a period of rapid social change, Congress should once again permit the President to use his Executive Office appropriations to fund committees dealing with experimental programs.

Chapter IV

FAIR HOUSING

On the evening of November 20, 1962, President John F. Kennedy went before the cameras at 6 P.M. for a televised news conference that was dominated by the Cuban crisis. He had chosen this time to announce Executive Order No. 11063, which specifically established an official national public policy of nondiscrimination in federally assisted housing. The order prohibited discrimination in the sale, lease, or use of future housing constructed by the federal government or guaranteed under the Federal Housing Administration or Veterans Administration programs. It created a President's Committe on Equal Opportunity in Housing to help implement this policy.

Kennedy's action was the fulfillment of a campaign promise after a delay of twenty-two months. It was also the culmination of more than two decades of effort by various groups to secure such an order. It was followed two years later by congressional action that partially superseded the order by prohibiting discrimination in federally assisted public housing (Title VI, Civil Rights Act of 1964). Subsequently, the Civil Rights Act of 1968 extended the statutory ban to the remainder of the housing covered by Executive Order No. 11063.

Pattern of Discrimination

When Kennedy assumed the Presidency, the government had been a participant in housing programs for three decades. During this time only minor gains toward nondiscrimination in housing had been made through a few administrative rules and regulations, and yet the national government had become perhaps the most important factor in the national housing picture.

Federal housing programs include both publicly owned and operated housing and financial assistance for private housing. As a matter of fundamental policy, these programs from the beginning have operated through private industry or local public authorities. But by the time the federal government entered the housing scene, racial discrimination had already become the practice of the private housing industry. Therefore, government agencies sustained discriminatory practices by leaving patterns of occupancy to local determination. In its 1961 report the U.S. Commission on Civil Rights noted that "the private housing and home finance industries . . . profit from the benefits that the Federal Government offers—and on racial grounds deny large numbers of Americans equal housing opportunity." The report continues, "At all levels of the housing and home finance industries—from the builder and the lender to the real estate broker, and often even the local housing authority—Federal resources are utilized to accentuate this denial."[1]

Thus the major racial issue in the federal housing program has been the extent to which the national government should control the discriminatory practices of private business and local public agencies. As a practical matter, policies with regard to the housing of racial minorities depended on the agencies involved. Although the Civil Rights Act of 1866, still in effect, stipulates that "all citizens of the United States shall have the same rights in every state and territory, as is enjoyed by white citizens thereof, to . . . purchase . . . real and personal property . . . " no specific nondiscrimination provision had been included in any federal legislation that authorized financial assistance to housing. On this basis, housing agency administrators showed a reluctance to deal with the problem of discrimination internally. For example, B. C. Bovard, as general counsel of the FHA, which insures loans for private housing, said in 1951: "I know of nothing in the National Housing Act or in the Rules and Regulations thereunder which would authorize the Commissioner to require that mortgagors disregard racial considerations in the selection of their tenants."[2]

In publicly owned housing, a program which was started in a limited way in 1934, the practice was to assure that minorities had an equitable share of the units, even though the decision as to segregation was left to the local public housing authorities. The Public Works Administration Housing Division (later incorporated into the Public Housing Administration under the Housing Act of 1937) set the precedent of utilizing racial relations specialists to assist in the formulation of overall agency policy and procedure as it affected racial minorities.[3] In 1951 the Public Housing Administration's *Low Rent Housing Manual* required that equitable provision be made for all racial groups in low-rent housing projects in order to be eligible for PHA assistance, but continued to leave the decision on segregation to local authorities.

On the other hand, the Federal Housing Administration, established under the National Housing Act of 1934, initially encouraged racial segregation on the theory that property values in a "white" neighborhood deteriorate when Negroes move into it. The 1938 *Underwriting Manual* said: "If a neighborhood is to retain stability, it is necessary that properties shall continue to be occupied by the same social and racial classes." To this end the manual recommended use of restrictive covenants to ensure against "inharmonious racial groups" and even provided a model covenant for inclusion in real estate contracts. Prompted by criticism from various groups, the FHA removed all direct references to race in the 1947 edition of the manual,[4] but the Commissioner wrote to employees in field offices that the change in language did not remove the responsibility to take into account factors of the local market that reflect upon value.[5]

The following year, in 1948, the Supreme Court held in *Shelley* v. *Kraemer* that the enforcement of racially restrictive covenants by state courts constituted a denial of equal protection of the law. In the same year the Court held in *Hurd* v. *Hodge* that a restrictive covenant was unenforceable in the federal court of the District of Columbia on the basis of the 1866 Civil Rights Act. Nineteen months later, the Federal Housing Administration reluctantly ruled that it would not insure loans on property which had a racial covenant *recorded* after February 15, 1950.[6] The FHA made this alteration in its underwriting regulations under pressure, and the Justice Department, rather than the housing agency, announced the change.[7] In doing so, Philip B. Perlman, Solicitor General, stated that President Truman "has been working on this matter for some time, and is most happy over the result of his efforts."

In addition to the racial covenant restriction, the 1949 *Underwriting Manual* stipulated that the racial composition of a neighborhood "is not a consideration in establishing eligibility." Despite these new regulations, the FHA continued to insure mortgages of builders and developers who were excluding racial or religious minorities, as long as covenants were not recorded. One of the best-known incidents was the Levittown project on Long Island. The FHA denied an application for loan insurance that included a racially restrictive covenant, but when the covenant was stricken from the application, the agency approved the guaranty and the developers proceeded to reject applications of

Negroes. The FHA Commissioner explained that he had "no authority to prevent racial discrimination in leasing or selling homes . . . after the developers built their houses.[8]

Pressure began during the Truman administration for an Executive order banning discrimination in housing. But the President did not overtly push nondiscrimination in housing, probably because he had urged Congress to enact comprehensive housing legislation for four years before the National Housing Act of 1949 passed.

When it was finally signed into law, the Act provided an important basis for nondiscriminatory policy in that it set for the first time a national housing goal of "a decent home and suitable living environment for every American family." President Kennedy emphasized later that "this objective cannot be fulfilled as long as some Americans are denied equal access to the housing market because of their race or religion."[9]

After the Housing Act passed, civil rights advocates—including the National Committee Against Discrimination in Housing, the National Association for the Advancement of Colored People, and some congressman,—urged the President to issue an Executive order banning discrimination in housing.[10] However, in addition to the chance of congressional reprisal against the housing program, Truman's advisory Committee on Civil Rights had not recommended Presidential action in this area and had split almost evenly on the proposal that Congress make nondiscrimination a condition for builders applying for federal financial assistance.[11] The White House staff considered the proposal so controversial that the President did not mention it in his Civil Rights message to Congress or in the proposed bill.[12] In fact, the staff discouraged congressional attention to discrimination in housing: "We are making progress in the practice of nondiscrimination in the field of housing as we are in other fields, by the use of administrative measures, far more rapidly than we will if we engage in legislative battles which arise when hard and fast clauses are introduced on the Hill."[13]

Shortly after Eisenhower became President, he established an Advisory Committee on Government Housing Policies under the chairmanship of Housing and Home Finance Administrator Albert M. Cole. The Committee made no recommendations regarding executive or legislative action with respect to minority housing in its report to the President in 1953.

In his Housing message to Congress in early 1954, Eisenhower indicated that during his administration also, action regarding racial discrimination in housing would be taken at the agency level. He said that "the administrative policies governing operations of the several housing agencies must be, and they will be, materially strengthened and augmented in order to assure equal opportunity for all of our citizens to acquire, within their means, good and well-located homes." Nevertheless, three times at news conferences during the next six months he was noncommittal when asked what steps had been taken to implement his message.

Actually, little had been done. Cole, whose appointment as Housing and Home Finance Administrator was not welcomed by some Negro groups,[14] was slower to act on the problem of minority housing than the White House would have liked.[15] Nevertheless, when Cole did call a meeting at the White House in July, 1954, to discuss the problem, no publicity was released for fear of jeopardizing the administration's high-priority housing bill (later enacted as the Housing Act of 1954), which was in conference committee at the time.[16] Furthermore, Eisenhower opposed tying the problem of civil rights to that of housing, although he did emphasize that he was determined not to allow use of public funds to foster racial discrimination in any area of national governmental activity.[17]

The pressure that had begun during the Truman administration for a fair housing Executive order continued through the Eisenhower administration, with recommendations coming in from many groups. For example, briefs were submitted to the President by the American Friends Service Committee, the National Urban League, the National Association for the Advancement of Colored People, and the National Committee Against Discrimination in Housing.[18] After releasing the 1959 report, the staff director of the U.S. Commission on Civil Rights submitted a proposed Executive order to the White House for consideration.[19] During the final months of 1959, the Housing and Home Finance Agency had the draft of this order under intense study. Norman P. Mason, who had succeeded Cole as Housing and Home Finance Administrator in 1959, was more active than his predecessor in pursuing a program of nondiscrimination in housing. However, he agreed with the White House that no Executive order should be issued on the subject.[20]

Therefore, by the time John F. Kennedy was inaugurated, the policy remained one of predominantly local control of occupancy patterns in federally assisted housing, even though the housing agencies had issued some regulations regarding discrimination.

Pressures on the Chief Executive

A national policy of nondiscrimination in housing could be carried out administratively, and consequently most of the public demand was for Executive action. The civil rights groups for the most part wanted to keep the issue out of congressional controversy. The American Jewish

Congress, for example, supported a proposal to establish a President's Committee on Housing Discrimination by Executive order, since this could be done without legislation and "we would not want to be caught in the trap of going back to the Congress of the United States and trying to pass legislation which would follow through on this."[21]

When Roy Wilkins of the NAACP was asked by the Commission on Civil Rights whether he preferred the executive or the legislative approach, he hedged, saying, "Well, . . . it is desirable, of course, that the Federal Government act in whatever way proves to be the most effective, and it could act without legislation if it had a firm and affirmative policy on this in the executive branch and if it would move to execute that policy."[22]

Civil rights groups insisted that the housing agencies had ample authority to issue regulations to prevent segregation in housing financed in whole or in part by federal funds. However, by 1961 the Federal Housing Administration, the Public Housing Administration, and the Urban Renewal Administration had made it clear that further steps to assure equal opportunity to all Americans would await Presidential or legislative direction.

The movement for a Presidential ban on discrimination in federally aided housing was led by the National Committee Against Discrimination in Housing, organized in 1950 with Robert C. Weaver as chairman and Charles Abrams as vice chairman. Weaver was later appointed by President Kennedy in 1961 as Housing and Home Finance Administrator and by President Johnson in 1966 as head of the new Department of Housing and Urban Affairs.

The National Committee Against Discrimination in Housing was an affiliation of thirty-seven major religious, labor, civil rights, and civic organizations, which acted both independently and collectively to secure a fair housing Executive order. On September 27, 1961, the NCDH met in Washington and opened a full-scale nationwide campaign for an order. It sent the President a proposed draft and an accompanying legal brief. NCDH Director Frances Levenson commented later that for more than two years these groups had to keep the same issue constantly before the public. At the same time they had to maintain a balance between putting relentless pressure on the President and avoiding antagonizing him. [23] When President Kennedy did issue Executive Order No. 11063, he acknowledged the NCDH's efforts and sent the Committee one of the pens used in signing the order.

Various study committees also recommended Presidential action to further open-occupancy policies in housing. In 1958 the Commission on Race and Housing, an independent, business-oriented citizens' group formed in 1955 to investigate the housing problems of minority groups, released the major findings of its three-year study, entitled *Where Shall We Live?* Its first proposal was for Presidential action to end discrimination in government housing activities. The Commission recommended that the President establish a committee to eliminate discrimination in federal housing and urban renewal programs.

This report was followed in 1959 by one from the U.S. Commission on Civil Rights that also favored a Presidential housing order. Then in October, 1961, the Civil Rights Commission released its second major set of housing recommendations, and again urged the President to issue an executive order stating "the national objective of equal opportunity in housing." In its 1961 report the Commission added that "for full effectiveness, an Executive Order should extend to all Federal agencies . . . which supervise the mortgage lending community."

Two of the Commission members, Robert S. Rankin and Robert G. Storey, dissented from this statement. Storey, head of the Southwestern Legal Center in Dallas, Texas, and former president of the American Bar Association, said that he was very much opposed to further intervention by the federal government into the affairs of private financial institutions engaged in the mortgage loan business.

In addition to the recommendations of interested groups and both private and governmental study committees, the two major parties pledged for the first time in 1960 to take action to prohibit discrimination in federally assisted housing. The Democratic Party platforms in 1952 and 1956 had included a general statement that all citizens should have equal opportunities for decent living conditions, but the 1960 platform contained a promise that the Chief Executive would act to end discrimination in federal housing programs, including federally assisted housing.

To offset the pressures from civil rights advocates, others (such as representatives of the real estate interests, Southern politicians, and some administrators in the housing agencies) opposed a fair housing Executive order. They argued that it would slow down the construction program and that the South would simply refuse federal aid; thus the minorities would be hurt by an order designed to aid them. The National Association of Home Builders sent a study to the President in July, 1962, emphasizing that new building would be sharply reduced if an Executive order were issued. The report indicated a minimum loss of three billion dollars on the gross national product, should racial discrimination in housing be prohibited.[24] The chairmen of both the House and the Senate subcommittees on housing also argued that an Executive order would have a bad, if not disastrous, effect on the federal housing program and on the whole housing market. Furthermore, housing agency spokesmen, anxious about the housing programs, expressed disapproval of a change in policy.[25]

Action by Congress

Even though most of the pressure was for an Executive order, civil rights proponents also attempted to get Congress to act. Beginning in 1949 members of both parties introduced a continuous flow of bills in one or the other house to end discrimination where federal funds were involved. However, none of these, and no antidiscrimination amendment to a housing bill, was ever reported out of committee. As a result, antidiscrimination amendments were offered to housing bills many times from the House and Senate floors. On one occasion during the Truman administration, a fair housing amendment passed the House, but a parliamentary maneuver eliminated it from the final bill.

The first major skirmish occurred when an antidiscrimination amendment was brought to a vote in the Senate during consideration of the Housing Act of 1949. Proponents of public housing charged that Republican Senators John W. Bricker of Ohio and Harry P. Cain of Washington offered the antisegregation amendment in order to defeat the legislation and place the liberals who supported both housing and civil rights in the awkward position of voting against the amendment in order to save the housing bill.

Civil rights groups themselves were mixed in their reaction to the amendment. Some opposed the Bricker amendment because of the possibility that it might kill the housing program. Charles Abrams, vice chairman of NCDH, wrote that the Cain-Bricker amendment, "proffered by the real estate lobby as part of its strategy to alienate southern support from the housing bill," if it succeeded, would "become the forerunner of a whole series of efforts to use the civil-rights issue as an instrument for killing off civil reform."[26]

On the other hand, the NAACP not only urged support for the Bricker amendment, but also requested a broader one to cover all federally aided public and private housing.[27] And the National Negro Council sent a resolution to the Republican and Democratic leadership in the Senate charging them to keep the civil rights pledges in their platforms at this first opportunity for a direct vote on the issue.[28]

The Cain-Bricker amendment was rejected on April 21, 1949, by a 49 to 31 vote, and the same day the housing bill passed the Senate, 57 to 13. In the House, antidiscrimination amendments to the housing bill were also rejected. Indeed, the only time an antidiscrimination amendment to housing legislation ever passed either house was in August, 1949, during House consideration of a bill to amend the National Housing Act. At that time an amendment to prohibit discrimination "by segregation or otherwise" in housing was approved by a teller vote of 77 to 57 about two minutes before debate on the bill and all its amendments was to close. To forestall final action, the Democratic chairman of the House Currency and Banking Committee, Brent Spence of Kentucky, moved that the Committee of the Whole rise, and this was agreed to by an 86 to 83 teller vote. The following day Spence offered a committee substitute that eliminated the antidiscrimination amendment adopted the previous day, and the amended bill passed. However, the Senate never took action on the bill.

The House again rejected antidiscrimination amendments during consideration of the Housing Act of 1950 and the Defense Housing and Community Facilities and Services Act of 1951. In the latter case, Congressman Abraham J. Multer consulted the FHA before the bill reached the floor. FHA officials told him that the agencies involved had issued regulations prohibiting discrimination and that similar regulations would be issued upon enactment of the Defense Housing Act. They assured him that no amendment was needed.[29] Accordingly, Multer opposed the nondiscrimination amendment offered by his fellow New Yorker Jacob Javits, with the argument that since FHA regulations covered the situation, the amendment was unnecessary and might defeat the bill. The Javits amendment was rejected on division, 79 to 57.

When Multer later learned that the FHA was not prohibiting discrimination in FHA-aided projects, he wrote to Truman. Multer urged the President to issue an Executive order prohibiting discrimination under existing housing legislation and to issue another order, simultaneously with his signing of the Defense Housing Act, which would apply to all titles of that bill.[30] Charles Murphy and Philleo Nash of the White House staff tried to alleviate the problem by getting the FHA to issue new regulations.[31] The FHA refused, however; and Raymond Foley, Housing and Home Finance Administrator, eventually issued a policy statement on November 15, 1951, that the Defense Housing Act would be administered to meet the needs of eligible persons of all races.[32] Foley sent a copy of the statement to Multer, and in an accompanying letter he emphasized that the federal government could and would insure mortgage loans covering residential property which the owners voluntarily chose to operate on a nonsegregated basis, and that the government would actively encourage and assist the development of such housing projects.[33]

The next major skirmish over a nondiscrimination provision occurred during consideration of the Housing Act of 1954. Ten days after a court decision that segregation in public housing by a municipal ordinance violated the Fourteenth Amendment,[34] South Carolina Democrat Burnet R. Maybank, chairman of the Senate Banking and Currency Committee, withdrew his support of public housing. He offered an amendment to bar any new public housing construction, but this was rejected by voice vote. Subsequently, Representatives Adam Clayton Powell and Jacob Javits proposed nondiscrimination amendments to the Housing Act of 1954, but both were rejected. Javits's would have empowered the FHA Commissioner to issue antidiscrimination regulations.

During congressional debate on the Housing Act of 1959, Powell offered a nondiscrimination amendment to a substitute bill that came to a vote first, but the amendment was rejected 138 to 48. After the defeat of the substitute bill, Powell did not propose his amendment to the committee bill as he had promised, because of the Democrats' conviction that the Republicans planned to support the amendment in order to defeat the housing legislation.

Thus by the time Kennedy assumed the Presidency, Congress for more than a decade had rejected antidiscrimination amendments to housing bills, frequently on grounds that they would defeat housing legislation. Because of this legislative history against incorporating antiracial requirements in housing laws, some Congressmen had misgivings as to the legal authority of the President to enforce such requirements by Executive order.[35]

The Kennedy Housing Order

In August, 1960, presidential candidate John F. Kennedy promised that, if elected, he would issue a fair housing Executive order. He repeated this pledge several times during the campaign. Not only did he emphasize that a "stroke of the presidential pen" could end discrimination in federally assisted housing, but he challenged President Eisenhower to issue the order and thereby effect the unanimous recommendation of the Civil Rights Commission in its 1959 report.

Since Kennedy had already made the decision to issue the Executive order, after his inauguration the two major remaining questions concerned its timing and scope. The story of the twenty-two month delay in redeeming the campaign promise reveals Kennedy's attempt to issue the order when it least endangered other matters important to him as President, and at the same time, to meet the needs and demands of an important segment of his constituency. Kennedy received 68 to 78 percent of the Negro vote, according to Gallup and Harris polls. Had only whites gone to the polls in 1960, Nixon would have taken 52 percent of the vote.

One of President Kennedy's first acts was to appoint Dr. Robert C. Weaver, then the chairman of the NCDH and chairman of the board of the NAACP, as Housing and Home Finance Administrator. The President delayed the Executive order awaiting the action of Congress on Weaver's nomination.[36] The appointment was confirmed February 11, 1961, and meant that the President now had a Housing and Home Finance Administrator who was committed to prohibition of racial discrimination in housing. During the hearing before the Senate Banking and Currency Committee, Weaver affirmed his support of an antibias mandate, but asserted that action was the President's responsibility. Kennedy then delayed issuing the order until Congress acted on his housing bill, which was dependent on Southern sponsorship in both Senate and House and which would be administered by Weaver.[37] The Housing Act of 1961 passed, but the first session of the 87th Congress did not bring to a final vote the President's recommendation (transmitted to Congress in April) for the establishment of a Department of Urban Affairs.

The President also decided, according to Theodore Sorensen, his special counsel, to wait for the housing report that was due in the fall of 1961 from the Civil Rights Commission and also to take more time for a carefully drafted Executive order. In the meanwhile, he gave priority to an Executive order on fair employment practices and to administrative actions on voting, education, and other areas.[38]

Arthur M. Schlesinger, Jr., special assistant to the President, has written that Kennedy intended to issue the order when Congress adjourned in the fall of 1961.[39] There was considerable speculation at that time that an order was imminent. On November 27 the *New York Times* carried a front-page story that the Executive order was on the President's desk and that a decision to sign it prior to the opening of Congress was expected momentarily. Such timing, according to the *Times's* sources, would provide "moderate" Southern legislators an opportunity to go on record against the order in their home states without jeopardizing key legislation. However, the same story added that White House aides who were charged with lobbying administration bills through Congress considered such an order an invitation to Southern retaliation. One suggested alternative was to push ahead with the upgrading of Weaver's agency into a Cabinet-level Department of Housing and Urban Affairs.

The elevation of the Housing and Home Finance Agency to Cabinet status was an important item in the 1962 legislative program, and the only hope for passage rested with two relatively moderate Alabamians who handled housing legislation in their respective chambers, Senator John Sparkman and Congressman Albert Rains.[40] Their support, and that of their Southern colleagues, would not be forthcoming if the fair housing Executive order were issued first. The President, according to Sorensen, decided that the achievement of Weaver's elevation, as well as the substantive value of the bill, was sufficiently important to merit another delay.[41]

Weaver was reported to prefer the order to the bill, but to have agreed that if the President's strategy could obtain both, more delay would not be intolerable.[42] Then on December 28, newspapers picked up the story that the President had decided to delay the order temporarily. When asked about the proposed order at a January 15, 1962, news conference, Kennedy answered that he had said he would issue the order when he considered it to be in the public interest. "We are proceding in a way which will maintain a consensus, and which will advance this cause," he added.

Congress convened on January 10, and the House Rules Committee killed the Urban Affairs bill by a 9 to 6 margin. Kennedy redrafted the measure as Reorganization Plan No. 1 of 1962 and sent it to Congress January 30. In answer to a planted news conference question, he announced his intention of naming Weaver to the post.[43] This fact was no secret on the Hill, but the President wanted the public to know. However, instead of putting the Republicans on the spot, as intended, the plan hardened the GOP-Dixie coalition's resistance and the reorganization measure was lost. This approach "was so obvious it made them mad," the President later commented.[44]

If Kennedy had issued the order immediately after the defeat of the Urban Affairs bill, he might have been charged with using the Executive order for political retaliation. Also, the rest of his program was in trouble. At his July 5, 1962, news conference he answered, in response to a question about the order: "I will announce it when we think it would be a useful and appropriate time."

Some thought the "appropriate" time might be September. Reports circulated in the fall of 1962 that the President might announce the housing order during the centennial of the Emancipation Proclamation. However, Congress had not completed action on the trade bill and the foreign aid appropriation bill—both needing Southern votes.

An October 22 front-page story in the *New York Times* predicted that the order would be issued after election day and before the end of the year, because to issue it before the election might "look like a mere political gesture." The *Times* also reported that some officials believed the order would do the administration more harm than good politically, since it might anger conservatives, while the voters it appealed to were Democrats already.

In addition, the President may have been concerned that the order might slow business recovery during the fall by delaying new construction. The National Association of Home Builders, which had polled its members regarding their building plans if an Executive order were issued, predicted a severe economic decline.[45] Other opponents of a racial ban also claimed that a Presidential order would have an adverse economic effect and "would serve in a measure to undo a larger part of the great accomplishments that have been made through the many housing measures."[46] Senator A. Willis Robertson, chairman of the Senate Banking Committee, warned that the order would curtail housing construction "by anywhere from 25 to 50 percent."[47] Since residential construction totaled 1.4 million new homes in 1962, it provided strong support for business generally. Finally, the strong federal action required to ensure admission of a Negro student to the University of Mississippi ended any possibility for the order before the November elections.[48]

Theodore Sorensen has written that "the President . . . looked for the least divisive approach when he considered civil rights action," and that in this instance, the President's desire was to make a low-keyed announcement.[49] At last he chose the time: the evening of November 20, the night before the long Thanksgiving weekend. He announced it at a 6 P.M. news conference which was dominated by the Cuban crisis. During the conference only one reporter asked about the order, and that was to learn why it had been delayed so long. The President answered: "I said that I would issue it at the time when I thought it was in the public interest and now is the time."

In addition to timing, the other major decision with regard to the order was its coverage. Proponents of an Executive order on housing generally agreed that to be meaningful, it should include federally owned housing, public housing, urban renewal, and housing financed with the aid of FHA-insured or VA-guaranteed loans.[50] Beyond this, however, the coverage was uncertain. At least as late as September 17, 1962, the President was reported to be undecided whether to include conventional loans and mortgages by financial institutions regulated by federal agencies, as recommended by the Civil Rights Commission.[51] He finally decided not to. According to news reports, Kennedy was concerned about the impact on home building if almost all avenues to mortgage credit were closed to persons rejecting a special contract clause on race. Some advisers, however, insisted that these lenders be included to ensure equity and to plug all loopholes.[52]

The argument for including conventional financing was that federal deposit insurance of banks and savings and loan associations is, in effect, federal aid to their lending. But some officials concluded that this was a rather tenuous connection which could be challenged.[53] Nicholas deB. Katzenbach, Deputy U.S. Attorney General, later told a housing conference that authority to deny membership in the FDIC system to private banks which practice discrimination is less clear than the sanctions provided in the order. He explained that "with respect to litigation, it is essential that the first cases be strong legally." "Favorable court decisions," he said, "are vitally important to establish precedents for subsequent court action."[54] Furthermore, had federally insured financial institutions been included, more than 90 percent of housing construction would have been covered. According to Justice Department officials, this would have led to "very serious enforcement problems."[55] The Justice Department supported the view that the experience gained in implementing the order, which covered about 25 percent of all homes built in the United States, could provide guidance for possible future expansion, and that this would enable the government to make step-by-step progress in the field.[56] The disadvantages of initially covering virtually 90 percent of housing construction thus outweighed the advantage of closing loopholes.

Another decision with regard to coverage was whether or not to make the order retroactive. Reports were that the administration considered it unfair to reopen contracts signed in good faith and was inclined to let the courts sort out any individual rights under old contracts.[57] The President decided that the order would apply to future housing constructed under federal aid agreements executed *after* the order's effective date. Thus, existing housing that previously received federal assistance, housing that was still receiving federal assistance, and even housing that had not yet been built were unaffected if the assistance agreement was made before the date of November 20, 1962. Such housing was covered to the extent that the housing agencies were directed to use their "good offices" and to take other action permitted by law (including litigation, if required) to promote nondiscriminatory practices in housing previously provided with federal financial assistance.

Reaction to the order was mixed. Although it was not as broad in coverage as many civil rights leaders had hoped, the National Committee Against Discrimination in Housing considered it a "qualified victory." The NCDH did not expect revolutionary changes, but they did anticipate the gradual opening of housing opportunities as a result of the order. They agreed that the moral impact would be one of the most important effects, and one that could ultimately have a far-reaching influence on the housing market.[58]

Some critics insisted that the order was too limited and too late. Loren Miller, NCDH vice president, believed that "the Order's very lateness reduces its effectiveness." He said, "Had precisely the same order been issued in the 1930's or the 1940's—perhaps even in the early 1950's—it would have . . . substantially curtailed the mushroom growth of the all-white developments that ring our cities."[59] The civil rights advocates who conducted a March on Washington for Jobs and Freedom on August 28, 1963, demanded a new Executive order banning discrimination in all housing supported by federal funds. However, when President Kennedy was questioned at a news conference September 12 about reports that he was considering a more sweeping order, he answered: "No, the order we now have is the one we plan to stand on."

Other critics said the order was undesirable and harmful to the economy.[60] Some Southern senators announced that they would try to have it reversed by statute on the grounds that it represented "an audacious usurpation of power" reserved to Congress by the Constitution.[61] The argument regarding legality was based on the constitutional grant to Congress of the power to appropriate funds. The Southerners claimed that this grant implicitly empowered Congress to fix the conditions of the money's use.[62]

However, Kennedy said in the preamble to the order that the President, in faithfully executing the laws of the United States which authorize federal financial assistance for housing, "is charged with an obligation and duty to assure that those laws are fairly administered and that benefits thereunder are made available to all Americans without regard to their race, color, creed, or national origin." And despite the protest over legality, when a bill to repeal Executive Order No. 11063 was introduced in the House, it was referred to the Committee on Banking and Currency and died there.

Another objection to using Executive orders or statutes to assure equality of housing opportunity was the interference with individual property rights.[63] For example, the National Association of Real Estate Boards in 1963 adopted a "Property Owner's Bill of Rights" that included "the right to occupy and dispose of property without governmental interference in accordance with the dictates of his conscience."[64] Of course, much of the impact of the new policy upon the individual homeowner depended upon the implementation of the order.

Application of the Housing Policy

Executive Order No. 11063 placed primary responsibility for obtaining compliance with the nondiscrimination policy on the various executive agencies that administered housing programs. The agencies were instructed to issue regulations, adopt policies and procedures, and enforce nondiscrimination—first through conciliation, and then through sanctions. The sanctions included canceling the contract for federal aid, barring the violator from further aid, and refusing to approve a lending institution as a beneficiary under any program. Agencies were also authorized to refer violations to the Attorney General for civil or criminal action under existing laws. The order established the President's Committee on Equal Opportunity in Housing to coordinate federal activities under the order, to examine all agency rules, to make recommendations, to report to the President, and to encourage educational programs by private groups.

Pursuant to the Executive order, the FHA and VA, which together guarantee about 25 percent of mortgages on new homes, issued regulations exempting one- and two-family, owner-occupied housing from the antidiscrimination pledge. This ruling, made on November 28, 1962, followed the precedent set by state and local fair housing laws to avoid complications in enforcement. Policing individual deals, according to officials, is extremely difficult and tangled with red tape.[65]

On January 11, 1962, the President appointed David L. Lawrence, former governor of Pennsylvania, as chairman of the Committee. Months then passed before appointment of the public members. Impatient with the delay, the National Committee Against Discrimination in Housing held a press conference in Washington April 26, and released a statement that attacked the slow progress in implementing the Executive order. The statement listed four "critical deficiencies": (1) delay in formal organization of the committee, (2) no public or internal information program underway, (3) no indication of serious exploration of ways to effectively use the "good offices" section, and (4) underutilization of the intergroup relations service by the housing agencies. The civil rights spokesmen concluded that "neither the broad spirit nor the limited letter of the Order is being made a reality." [66]

Three weeks later, on May 16, the President appointed the eight public members. Chairman Lawrence explained that the delay in formal organization of the committee was due to the fact that security checks of Presidential appointees take as long as two or three months.[67]

The Executive order was in effect only one year under President Kennedy. In its 1963 report, the Civil Rights Commission felt that it was too early to assess the effect of the order and consequently made no recommendations on housing. Housing Administrator Weaver stated in 1963, however, that it was apparent no major changes had occurred.[68] Nevertheless, the housing agencies at least showed an intention to apply the sanctions in implementing the order. The Veteran's Administration stopped doing business with a Chicago real estate broker in April, 1963, and a Florida builder in July, 1963, because of their discriminatory practices.[69]

Subsequent Congressional and Executive Action

In 1964 Congress passed legislation that in effect validated Executive Order No. 11063. Having decided as a candidate on a strategy of Executive action in the field of civil rights, President Kennedy had sought no major civil rights legislation for two years. Then in the spring of 1963 he decided that public interest in civil rights legislation had made congressional passage at least possible. On June 19 he sent proposals to Congress that expanded the pattern his Executive actions had started. These differed only slightly from the Civil Rights Act passed the following year and signed by President Johnson. Kennedy, at the suggestion of congressional leaders, added a broad authorization to withhold federal funds from any program that practiced racial discrimination, in order to prevent certain congressmen from offering nondiscrimination amendments to programs they hoped to defeat.[70]

Although Title VI of the Civil Rights Act of 1964 prohibited discrimination in federally assisted programs or activities, it excluded programs involving "a contract of insurance or guaranty." Therefore, Executive Order No. 11063 continued to apply to the FHA mortgage insurance programs and VA-guaranteed loans, while Title VI covered federally assisted public housing.

When Lyndon B. Johnson assumed the Presidency, he shifted the emphasis from Executive action to legislation and requested, for the first time, a federal open housing law in his State of the Union message, January 12, 1966. The proposal was included in an omnibus civil rights bill sent to Congress April 28, 1966. The House passed an amended version of the bill on August 9, but a filibuster killed it in the Senate.

Johnson renewed his request for fair housing legislation in his message on civil rights sent to Congress the following February. He modified the housing provision to the extent that the ban on discrimination would go into effect by progressive stages, the first stage to cover housing already included in the 1962 Executive order. This still did not make the proposal palatable, and the House on August 16, 1967, passed a civil rights bill that contained only a civil rights protection provision.

In the Senate, proponents of the administration's package introduced the sections of the bill as separate measures in an attempt to improve the chances for some of the provisions. Minnesota Democrat Walter Mondale introduced the open housing provision on February 6, 1968, even though proponents, as well as opponents, of open housing did not anticipate favorable action in 1968. But in one of the legislative surprises of the century, the Senate adopted a cloture motion to limit debate on the amended bill, which included a housing section.

The final obstacle in the legislative history of fair housing was overcome when the House on April 10 accepted the Senate amendments to the original House-passed civil rights bill. On April 11, 1968, President Johnson signed the measure, which included an open housing provision that was to cover 80 percent of all housing by 1970, when it would be fully in effect.

Conclusion

After his nomination, presidential candidate John F. Kennedy decided to utilize executive resources as the best immediate hope for civil rights progress. This approach fitted his conception of an activist President,[71] and furthermore, the 1957 and 1960 civil rights debates had left him pessimistic about further progress in Congress.[72]

The controversy over the housing program largely eliminated any prospect of Congress adding a nondiscrimination provision to housing bills. Consequently, most of the pressure for national action to prohibit discrimination in housing was on the executive branch.

As a candidate, Kennedy not only promised Executive action regarding civil rights, but pledged to issue an Executive order banning discrimination in federally assisted housing. Since he had already selected the alternative of the Executive order as the instrument for ending discrimination in housing, the remaining decisions to be made about it when Kennedy became President were those of timing and content. Unlike Presidents Truman and to some extent Eisenhower, he was not handicapped by reluctance on the part of officials who would administer the policy, for he had appointed a Housing and Home Finance Administrator who was deeply committed to open occupancy. However, despite the campaign promise and growing criticism from civil rights advocates, the order was not issued during the first twenty-two months of his administration. Political strategy played the controlling part in this delay. Advised that the order was not likely to attract many new voters, the President waited to issue it until he thought it was least likely to jeopardize his other programs in Congress.

In spite of previous refusals to add nondiscrimination provisions to housing bills, Congress tacitly approved the President's action by failing to pass conflicting legislation. Furthermore, Congress in effect validated the Executive order with subsequent legislation.

This chapter has illustrated several of the factors that may influence a President to act by Executive order on a controversial problem:

(1) public pressure for Executive action;
(2) the personal value choices of the President;
(3) the failure of the executive departments to adopt an adequate policy and yet the possibility of accomplishing the goal administratively;
(4) the failure of Congress to enact legislation;
(5) and the desire to avoid embroiling the issue in congressional controversy, with the possibility of a defeat.

Chapter V

TOOL FOR POLICY-MAKING

From the montage of policy-making in the American political system, this book has attempted to isolate one part—policy-making by Presidential Executive order—and to determine the factors that prompt the use of that instrument for the "authoritative allocation of values"[1] in our society. No effort was made to develop a checklist of all the variables that affect Presidential decision-making. In fact, all the influences on any one significant decision are probably indeterminable. Rather, the purpose in studying several decisions made by five Presidents was to examine the recurring ingredients that, when intermixed, prompt Presidents to make policy by Executive order.

Determining Factors

Preliminary to—or at least, coincident with—a choice between alternative means for securing a policy objective is the decision to act at all. The factors or forces that converge to influence a President in making this choice include his own values, his awareness of a specific problem and a demand for its solution, his perception of the political ramifications of action, and the ability or willingness of other policy-making institutions to act on their own initiative.

The President's personal values, and the ways in which he perceives the national interest and his constitutional responsibilities, form the underpinning for Presidential decision-making. Presidents Roosevelt, Truman, Eisenhower, Kennedy, and Johnson each were committed to the general value of equality of treatment and opportunity for all. Consequently, they were more receptive to specific policy proposals than they would have been had they opposed efforts to further the cause of civil rights.

However, they differed in their views of the Presidential role. Eisenhower was the only one of the five to approach the Presidency in the tradition of Executive restraint. Claiming no constitutional prerogatives for the executive branch, he was concerned about restoring confidence between the President and Congress. This no doubt made him less responsive to proposals for exercising independent constitutional authority for making policy. As we have noted, his two civil rights Executive orders were to some extent forced by the commitments of a preceding administration. Of the other four Presidents, who all belonged to the tradition of Executive activism, only Roosevelt did not seek active participation by the federal government in the field of civil rights.

Another factor which may influence a President to act is his awareness of a specific problem that requires national governmental action for its solution. In the day-to-day press of events, if the President is to take action, a general value (such as civil rights) must be converted into a more specific objective (such as military desegregation). This conversion may be performed by special-interest groups or various advisory bodies. For example, some interested groups (such as the Commission on Race and Housing), as well as a number of government committees (such as the President's Committee on Civil Rights), made special studies of one or more of the three issues of military desegregation, fair employment practices, and open housing. They included specific recommendations for Executive action in their reports to the President. Likewise, the importance of the President's staff in recommending specific opportunities for action should not be overlooked.

However, a Presidential decision is not invoked simply by bringing a particular problem to his attention; demand for a national governmental solution to that problem is another necessary force. For years special-interest groups, such as the National Council for a Permanent FEPC and the National Committee Against Discrimination in Housing, exerted pressure on the President and Congress for national bans on discrimination. In addition, both major political parties responded to civil rights interests by pledging to support various objectives—for example, fair employment practices legislation. And members of both parties introduced in Congress a continuous stream of bills on all three issues discussed here.

In weighing these demands, the President is intensely conscious of his sources of support. If he goes too far in suggesting policy goals, he becomes separated from some of his supporters. Yet if he stands still, he will surely alienate certain interests that could provide assistance. President Truman, for example, was aware that the Negro vote might be significant in the pivotal states in the 1948 election. Therefore, political party advantage was a controlling factor in his decision to desegregate the military and ban discrimination in government employment. President Kennedy was cognizant of his political debt to the Negro in the election of 1960 and of his promises in that campaign to ban discrimination in housing. These were important factors in his decision to issue the fair housing order.

In addition to a consideration of political ramifications, the inaction of other policy-makers frequently forces an issue to the President's desk. The reluctance of others to act may be at the administrative level: a program's executives may be unwilling or unable to put a policy into effect. This was true with regard to housing, for the few antidiscrimination rules and regulations adopted by the housing agencies had little effect. Furthermore, without a Presidential or congressional directive, some administrators showed a reluctance to interfere with the local control of occupancy patterns. In the case of the armed services, the Selective Service Act of 1940 stipulated nondiscrimination in the selection and training of men. Yet this was not interpreted as forbidding segregated units, but rather as requiring that Negroes be inducted in a proportion equal to their distribution in the general population. Therefore, further governmental action was needed to desegregate the military in the 1940's, especially since the "separate-but-equal" doctrine was not overturned by the Supreme Court until 1954.

On the other hand, it may be congressional failure to enact legislation that prompts Presidential decision. This can be noted in the history of fair employment practices. For a period of more than two decades Congress refused to legislate on employment practices, even though members of both political parties introduced a steady flow of bills in both houses.

These, then, are some of the major forces that impinge upon the President. All these factors, however, must pass through the filter of Presidential perspective. If he does decide to seek an authoritative policy, his two major alternatives are the formal Executive order and the recommendation of legislation to Congress. The choice between these hinges on (1) the relative importance of his various goals, (2) the degree to which his program can be implemented administratively, (3) the chances for enactment of legislation, and (4) the effect that Presidential pressure or action will have on other executive programs being considered by Congress. For example, legislation was not necessary in order to establish a nondiscrimination policy in federally aided housing. Consequently, none of the Presidents risked endangering housing legislation (which was also a matter of high priority) by pushing for statutory nondiscrimination provisions. Furthermore, a pessimistic view regarding the chances for any civil rights legislation, and concern over possible congressional reprisal on other executive programs, prompted President Kennedy, despite his campaign promises, to drop civil rights recommendations from his legislative program for two and one-half years after his inauguration.

Weighing the considerations listed above, the President may select the Executive order as the instrument for action in four types of situations. First, he may issue an order when Executive, rather than legislative, action is being demanded. This was the case with Roosevelt's FEPC orders. Second, he may select the Executive order when he can carry out the policy administratively and wants to avoid involving it in congressional controversy. Truman did this with regard to military desegregation. Third, if a politically important segment of the American public is demanding legislation, and if the President considers the risk of congressional defeat or reprisal to be too great, he may issue an Executive order rather than use his leadership to secure congressional action. President Kennedy's order to establish the Committee on Equal Employment Opportunity illustrates this point. Finally, the President may request legislation and then issue an Executive order if Congress does not respond with a law. President Truman's Executive orders on fair employment practices are an example of this situation.

A President will not attempt to publicize an Executive order if he wishes to avoid controversy that might create public resistance or might cause congressional reprisal against other programs. This was clearly the case when President Kennedy issued the fair housing order. On the other hand, if political party advantage is an important factor in issuing the order, then the President will announce it at a time and in a manner to attract attention. President Truman followed this course with the military desegregation and government fair employment practices orders.

Effectiveness

Another question examined in this study was the effectiveness of the Executive order as an instrument for policy-making. In relation to other types of officially binding decisions, the Executive order is subordinate to statutory law and the decisional law of the Supreme Court.

This, again, will be a factor that the President must weigh in considering whether to push Congress for legislation or to act on his own authority. The Executive order is subordinate, however, only if the other official policy-makers subsequently act. The President by Executive order can provide significant law in the void created by inaction.

In another sense, "effectiveness" means the degree to which the policies established by Executive orders accomplish their purpose. Armed services desegregation was indeed achieved. The goals of fair employment practices and open housing were not fully accomplished during the span of this study. Nevertheless, Executive orders in these areas did lay the groundwork for subsequent legislation. It is true that fair employment practices and fair housing statutes were a consequence of historical and political factors and did not arise from the necessity of regularizing the Executive orders by other types of action. But they indicated that the policies established by Executive order were successful to the extent that both political parties endorsed them and desired to increase their coverage. The Civil Rights Act of 1964 prohibited employment discrimination in the greater part of the nation's work force, and the Civil Rights Act of 1968 covered most of the nation's housing with an open occupancy provision. Furthermore, the Equal Employment Opportunity Commission, created by the Civil Rights Act of 1964, benefited from the many studies conducted by Presidential committees and from the pool of government employees experienced in coping with the problems of minority employment.

These Executive orders studied were also effective to the extent that the special-interest groups directly concerned were at least partially satisfied by the Presidential efforts. No organized opposition to any of the programs developed. On the contrary, the protest over armed forces segregation ceased. The interest groups concerned with fair employment practices and with open occupancy in housing expressed, if not complete satisfaction, at least qualified approval of the orders and the programs established to implement them.

It is sometimes said that Executive orders are ineffective in reaching the individual citizen. Certainly it is true that an Executive order does not direct a private citizen to cease a certain practice under penalty of fine or imprisonment. Executive orders are the President's directions to his subordinates. Nevertheless, if the President orders an agency to withhold contracts from private companies engaged in discriminatory employment practices, this has a direct effect upon the private citizen which is no different from a statutory prohibition of employment discrimination. Or if an individual purchases a home in a neighborhood of FHA housing, it makes little difference in its effect on him whether open occupancy was instituted by an Executive order or by a statute.

Constitutionality

Since the President can make significant and effective policy by Executive order, the question of the propriety of this exercise of Presidential power is raised. None of the Executive orders studied in the preceding chapters has been overruled by the Supreme Court. Their constitutionality may thus be temporarily assumed, but it can nonetheless be questioned.

The authority of the President, as Chief Executive and as Commander in Chief, to issue the orders banning discriminatory practices in government employment and in the armed forces is constitutionally incontestable. However, the President's authority to prohibit discriminatory practices in private enterprise operating under government contract and in federally aided housing is less clear. In these instances the President, under his interpretation of his responsibility to "take care that the laws be faithfully executed," established nondiscrimination requirements for receiving funds that had been appropriated by Congress. The fact that Congress had refused to pass legislation on these two subjects raises the question of whether or not it was proper for the President, under his implied constitutional authority, to have adopted such policies. In the Steel Seizure Case, in which a Presidential action by Executive order was declared unconstitutional, the Supreme Court relied heavily on congressional intent. However, in that instance Congress had provided alternate means for dealing with the type of emergency which the President met by issuing his order. This was not the case with regard to employment and housing discrimination. Congress had rejected legislation; but rejection is not necessarily equivalent to enactment of legislation of a different nature.

Although it may be objected that policy-making by Executive order is a dangerous usurpation of legislative power in the American governmental system, this does not seem to be the case. Unless "law" is defined as all enactments of Congress, then the other branches of government also make law. If one defines according to function rather than structure, then whoever makes policy is legislating—Congress through statutory law, the Supreme Court through decisional law, the President through executive law, and the departments and agencies through administrative law. The framers of the Constitution used the principle of separation of powers and the intricately contrived system of checks and balances to prevent the concentration of power in any one place. The overlapping of function that permits each branch to check and balance the tyrannical tendencies of the other is not endangered by the Presidential use of the Executive order. Rather, the use of the Executive order is confined to an area bounded by the judgement of the President and the support of the American public. Furthermore, an Executive order may be invalidated by Congress or overruled by the Supreme Court.

Another important consideration is the concept of representative government that is so fundamental to a democracy. Legislating is preeminently a representative function. The President, as well as Congress, represents the nation. Each is popularly elected and must return periodically to the voters for a performance review. Each has its own constituency—the President a national one and Congress a state and local one. Each affords interest groups access to the policy-making process, and frequently groups that have no access to one process will enjoy privileged access to the other.

Furthermore, there is evidence that a conscious effort was made to see that the Presidential committees charged with implementing the civil rights policies were themselves representative. For example, the Government Contract Committee was established as a fourteen-member group with eight public members, so that "this will give us a chance to make Negro, Jewish, industry, and labor appointments."[2] Similarly, a balance of interests was maintained for the Committee on Government Employment.[3]

Future of the Executive Order

The future of the Presidential Executive order as an instrument for policy-making lies in its use as a tool for solving complex policy problems. The Executive order provides a more flexible, adaptive framework than the relatively permanent molds of statutory law. This is evident from the successive Executive orders that broadened and strengthened the national government's program for enforcing fair employment practices.

The difficult issues that rend the fabric of our society require a variety of approaches. Obviously we have not found the answers to the civil rights dilemma. As various federal legislative programs are studied, they are found to be inadequate responses. Policies established by Executive order, however, can provide a good test, since a new policy may or may not have the desired effect. For example, it was uncertain if the ban on discrimination in federally aided housing would achieve its objectives. Many critics said that it would cause a shifting of financing to other sources or would have an adverse economic effect by holding back new building. These predictions proved unfounded, and Congress eventually covered by law the housing initially considered, but finally excluded, from the Executive order.

A traditional claim has been made that state and local governments provide "laboratories for experiment." Whether or not this is the case, a need also exists for experimental programs at the national level, programs without the full-scale commitment to a particular course that frequently comes with congressional enactments. As noted in the preceding pages, much of the success of the Presidential programs stemmed from the resourcefulness of the committees in the absence of specific appropriations and stronger enforcement powers. For example, one of the arguments for continuing the work of the Committee on Government Contract Compliance was that it was an inexpensive operation and meant "getting a great deal for very little."[4]

A more questionable practice is the use of the Executive order to control congressionally appropriated funds in such a way that congressional intent may be modified. The decision to use the government's economic power to enforce nondiscrimination practices in private employment through government contracts and in federally aided housing was an important new policy. The three Kennedy civil rights Executive orders were the first ones out of more than sixteen hundred orders issued since World War II to include a list of sanctions. Although the enforcement tools of canceling contracts and withholding funds were clearly backstops for previous Executive orders, these economic sanctions became an important part of the new policy, and were stated in the three orders themselves. The use of the economic power of the national government to enforce nondiscrimination practices was not adopted by Congress until the Civil Rights Law of 1964. Title VI of that law stipulates that no person in the United States shall be subjected to discrimination under any program or activity receiving federal financial assistance.

This is a precedent that could have considerable future impact. Since some of the funds appropriated by Congress may be distributed to state and local governments under conditions partly determined directly by a President's prerogative power, such use of the Executive order may provide an additional avenue for executive control of state and local administrative policy.

These conclusions regarding its future functions do not necessarily mean that the Executive order will be used with ever-increasing frequency. Presidents will continue to balance a multiplicity of considerations before issuing one. The same interacting influences of the President, Congress, the courts, special-interest groups, and voters will channel the use of the Executive order. Nevertheless, the President will doubtless continue to rely on the Executive order when he needs to move in advance of Congress in responding to wants acutely felt by interest groups and at least some congressmen, but insufficiently supported to overcome congressional inertia or opposition. This will be the case as long as congressional practices enable the thwarting of certain interests. For example, we have noted that no vote was ever taken on a fair employment practices bill in the Senate because of filibusters and the failure of cloture attempts. Similarly, in the House the Rules Committee never approved a fair employment practices bill for floor debate. Similar situations will undoubtedly arise in the future.

As lawmakers, Congress and the President are not passive vehicles equally accessible to all citizens. If a strong want or need gets clogged in the congressional machinery, a safety valve is a necessity in a viable political system. In ours, this function is sometimes performed by the courts and sometimes by the President. What is clear is that when a policy void exists because of congressional inaction, the system can provide law for the nation if the President does not hesitate to move in advance of Congress and if he has sufficient national support. The President, therefore, not only plays an important role in transforming interests and demands into laws, but on occasion also makes those laws.

Executive Orders on Civil Rights

The most important of the Presidential orders examined in this book are the following:

E.O. 8802 (June 25, 1941)—Stated the policy of elimination of discrimination in the employment of workers and established a Committee on Fair Employment Practice (FEPC) to carry out the nondiscrimination policy on all defense contracts.

E.O. 9346 (May 27, 1943)—Reconstituted the FEPC, charged it with preventing discrimination in the employment of persons in war industries and in government, and provided that contracting agencies of the federal government should include a nondiscrimination clause in all contracts.

E.O. 9664 (December 18, 1945)—Extended the authority of the Committee to study and make recommendations on employment discrimination in reconverted industries.

E.O. 9980 (July 26, 1948)—Declared a policy of nondiscrimination in government employment and established in the Civil Service Commission a Fair Employment Board with coordinating and advisory responsibilities.

E.O. 9981 (July 26, 1948)—Declared a policy of equality of treatment and opportunity for all persons in the armed forces and created the President's Committee on Equality of Treatment and Opportunity in the Armed Services.

E.O. 10308 (December 3, 1951)—Established the President's Committee on Government Contract Compliance to help make effective the non-discrimination clause in government contracts, since the FEPC had been killed by Congress. This is the only order listed that was established under statutory authority.

E.O. 10479 (August 13, 1953)—Revoked E.O. 10308 and established the Government Contract Committee to ensure that contractors or subcontractors complied with the nondiscrimination provisions required in government contracts.

E.O. 10557 (September 3, 1954)—Revised and strengthened the nondiscrimination clause mandatory in government contracts.

E.O. 10590 (January 18, 1955)—Replaced the Fair Employment Board with the President's Committee on Government Employment Policy, and charged it to strengthen the program to ensure nondiscrimination in government employment.

E.O. 10925 (March 6, 1961)—Replaced the Committee on Government Employment Policy and the Government Contract Committee with the President's Committee on Equal Employment Opportunity, whose purpose was to implement the nondiscrimination policies in both government employment and private employment under government contract.

E.O. 11063 (November 20, 1962)—Declared an official national public policy of nondiscrimination in federally assisted housing, to be coordinated by a President's Committee on Equal Opportunity in Housing.

E.O. 11114 (June 22, 1963)—Extended the authority of the President's Committee on Equal Employment Opportunity to include contracts for construction undertaken wholly or in part as a result of grant-in-aid programs.

E.O. 11197 (February 5, 1965)—Established the President's Council on Equal Opportunity to review and assist in coordinating the activities of all departments and agencies of the government that are directed toward the elimination of discrimination.

E.O. 11246 (September 24, 1965)—Abolished the President's Committee on Equal Employment Opportunity and transferred its functions to the Civil Service Commission and the Department of Labor.

Notes

INTRODUCTION

1. *The Negro in Federal Employment: The Quest for Equal Opportunity* (Minneapolis: University of Minnesota Press, 1967), p. 5.
2. Quoted in Theodore C. Sorensen, *Decision-Making in the White House: The Olive Branch or the Arrows* (New York: Columbia University Press, 1963), p. 10.

CHAPTER I

1. *Peters* v. *Hobby,* 349 U.S. 331, 350 (1955).
2. *Wolsey* v. *Chapman,* 101 U.S. 755, 770 (1879).
3. House Committee on Government Operations, *Executive Orders and Proclamations: A Study of a Use of Presidential Power* (Committee Print), 85th Cong., 1st Sess., 1957, p. 37.
4. *Youngstown Sheet & Tube Co.* v. *Sawyer* (Steel Seizure Case), 343 U.S. 579, 588 (1952).
5. *Armstrong* v. *United States,* 13 Wall. 154, 156 (1871).
6. *Jenkins* v. *Collard,* 145 U.S. 546, 560-561 (1891). Also consult Glendon A. Schubert, Jr., *The Presidency in the Courts* (Minneapolis: University of Minnesota Press, 1957), p. 314, n. 38, for a "partial list" of twenty cases that uphold Presidential orders as a source of law binding on both citizens and courts.
7. *United States* v. *Eaton,* 144 U.S. 677, 688 (1892).
8. *Cole* v. *Young,* 351 U.S. 536 (1956).
9. *Youngstown Sheet & Tube Co.* v. *Sawyer,* 343 U.S. 534 (1952).
10. *Little* v. *Barreme,* 2 Cr. 170 (1804).
11. *Hirabayashi* v. *United States,* 320 U.S. 81, 87, 88, 91 (1943).
12. *Fleming* v. *Mohawk Wrecking & Co.,* 331 U.S. 111, 116 (1947).
13. *United States* v. *Midwest Oil Co.,* 236 U.S. 459 (1915).
14. *Mississippi* v. *Johnson,* 4 Wall. 475 (1867).
15. *In re Neagle,* 135 U.S. 1 (1899).

CHAPTER II

1. *Integration in the Armed Services: A Progress Report Prepared by the Office of the Assistant Secretary of Defense* (Manpower and Personnel), January 1, 1955, p. 3.

2. House Armed Services Committee, *Hearings on Selective Service,* 80th Cong., 2d Sess., 1948, p. 6322; Senate Armed Services Committee, *Hearings On Universal Military Training,* 80th Cong., 2d Sess., 1948, p. 646.
3. In President's Committee on Equality of Treatment and Opportunity in the Armed Services, *Freedom to Serve* (1950), pp. 47-48. Hereafter cited as *Freedom to Serve.*
4. *Freedom to Serve,* p. 49.
5. "The Utilization of Negro Manpower in the Postwar Army," *Hearings on Universal Military Training,* pp. 651-661.
6. Memorandum, Milton Stewart to Robert Carr, April 7, 1947, Records of the President's Committee on Civil Rights, Harry S. Truman Library.
7. *Freedom to Serve,* pp. 33, 35.
8. Walter White, *How Far the Promised Land?* (New York: The Viking Press, 1955), p. 95.
9. Dennis D. Nelson, *The Integration of the Negro into the U.S. Army* (New York: Farrar, Straus & Young, 1951), pp. 12-13.
10. *Freedom to Serve,* p. 18. See Nelson, *op. cit.,* pp. 14-23.
11. This account is based on Lee Nichols, *Breakthrough on the Color Front* (New York: Random House, 1954), pp. 57-60.
12. Langston Hughes, *Fight for Freedom: The Story of the NAACP* (New York: W.W. Norton & Company, Inc., 1962), p. 90; Nichols, *op. cit.,* p. 62; White, *How Far the Promised Land?* p. 94.
13. Memorandum, Charles S. Thomas to the President, June 23, 1953, OF 142-A-4, Eisenhower Papers, Dwight D. Eisenhower Library.
14. *Freedom to Serve,* p. 20.
15. Some of the more important directives, letters, and other documents in the transition of Navy racial policy are reprinted in Nelson, *op. cit.,* pp. 197-226.
16. White, *How Far the Promised Land?* pp. 94-95.
17. Walter White, *A Man Called White* (New York: The Viking Press, 1948), pp. 190-193.
18. *New York Times,* June 20, 1944, 12:6.
19. *A Man Called White,* p. 330.
20. *Ibid.,* pp. 330-331. Cf. comments made by President Truman, in Louis W. Koenig (ed.), *The Truman Administration: Its Principles and Practice* (New York: New York University Press, 1956), pp. 117-121; *Public Papers of the Presidents of the United States: Harry S. Truman, 1947* (1963), pp. 98-99, 479-480. Hereafter cited as *Public Papers of the Presidents.*
21. *Hearings on Universal Military Training,* p. 682.
22. *Hearings on Selective Service,* p. 6420.
23. Hughes, *op. cit.,* p. 107.
24. Harry S. Truman, *Years of Trial and Hope* (Garden City, N.Y.: Doubleday & Company, Inc., 1956), p. 183.
25. Senator Wayne Morse, *Cong. Rec.,* 80th Cong., 2d Sess., 1948, XCIV, 7246.
26. *Hearings on Universal Military Training,* pp. 662-663.
27. *New York Times,* May 27, 1948, 1:3.
28. Walter Millis (ed.), *The Forrestal Diaries* (New York: The Viking Press, 1951), p. 439.
29. *Cong. Rec.,* 81st Cong., 2d Sess., 1950, XCVI, 8994.
30. *New York Times,* June 8, 1948, 1:5; 5:2.
31. "Civil Rights File," Spingarn Papers, Harry S. Truman Library.
32. Draft Memorandum, Clark Clifford to the Secretary of Defense, May 13, 1948, Nash Files, Harry S. Truman Library.
33. Truman, *Years of Trial and Hope,* pp. 206-208.
34. July 16, 1948, 3:2.
35. For the following account of the drafting of Executive Order No. 9981, based on interviews with Nash, Ewing, and Leva, I am indebted to Nichols, *op. cit.,* pp. 85-88.
36. *New York Times,* June 27, 1948, 56:1.
37. *Cong. Rec.,* 80th Cong., 2d Sess., 1948, XCIV, 9636.
38. In Nichols, *op. cit.,* p. 88.
39. July 27, 1948, 7:3.
40. *New York Times,* July 27, 1948, 4:3.

41. *Ibid.*, July 28, 1948, 5:1.
42. The *Washington Post*, July 28, 1948, 5:2.
43. Memorandum, Donald Dawson to the President, September 9, 1948, Nash Files, Harry S. Truman Library.
44. Transcript of Meeting, President's Committee on Equality of Treatment and Opportunity in the Armed Services, OF 1285-0, Truman Papers, Harry S. Truman Library.
45. *Freedom to Serve*, pp. 2-3.
46. This account is based on Paul I. Wellman, *Stuart Symington: Portrait of a Man with a Mission* (Garden City, N.Y.: Doubleday and Company, Inc., 1960), pp. 135-136.
47. *Freedom to Serve*, pp. 36-38.
48. Copy of Memorandum, Records of the President's Committee on Equality of Treatment and Opportunity in the Armed Services, Harry S. Truman Library. Hereafter cited as Truman Committee Records.
49. Memorandum, W. Stuart Symington to Chairman, Personnel Policy Board, Office of Secretary of Defense, April 30, 1949, and drafts of the Air Force Policy Statement and implementing directives, in Truman Committee Records.
50. Copies of the press release of May 11, 1949, and Air Force Letter 35-3, that contained the new policy, in Truman Committee Records.
51. *Freedom to Serve*, p. 39.
52. *Ibid.*, p. 27; Memorandum, marked "Confidential," Dan A. Kimball, Acting Secretary of the Navy to the Secretary of Defense, May 23, 1949, Truman Committee Records.
53. Nichols, *op. cit.*, p. 97.
54. Jacob K. Javits, House Armed Services Committee, *Hearings on Selective Service Act Extension*, 81st Cong., 2d Sess., 1950, p. 5222.
55. Copy of Memorandum, Gordon Gray to the Secretary of Defense, September 30, 1949, Truman Committee Records.
56. Memorandum, E. W. Kenworthy to Charles Fahy, November 22, 1949, Truman Committee Records.
57. Memorandums, Worthington Thompson to Mr. Bendetsen, September 9, 1949, and E. W. Kenworthy to Charles Fahy, October 29, 1949, Truman Committee Records.
58. Letter, Frank Pace, Jr., Secretary of the Army, to David K. Niles, Administrative Assistant to the President, February 21, 1951, OF 93-B, Truman Papers, Harry S. Truman Library. A copy of the instructions, Special Regulations No. 600-629-1, are included in this file.
59. *Hearings on Selective Service Act Extension*, p. 5149.
60. Memorandums for the President's Committee by Charles Fahy, February 1 and March 8, 1950, Truman Committee Records.
61. Memorandum, E. W. Kenworthy to Charles Fahy, November 22, 1949, Truman Committee Records.
62. *Freedom to Serve*, p. 82.
63. Eli Ginzberg, *The Negro Potential* (New York: Columbia University Press, 1956), pp. 86-87; Nichols, *op. cit.*, pp. 113-116; White, *How Far the Promised Land?*, p. 98.
64. Letter, President Truman to Charles Fahy, July 6, 1950, OF 1285-0, Truman Papers, Harry S. Truman Library.
65. Nichols, *op. cit.*, p. 134-135.
66. *New York Times*, June 22, 1950, 1:5, 6:3.
67. *Chicago Defender*, March 31, 1951, reprinted in *Cong. Rec.*, 82d Cong., 1st Sess., 1951, XCVII, A1936.
68. *How Far the Promised Land?*, p. 95.
69. Papers in OF 142-A-4, Eisenhower Papers, Dwight D. Eisenhower Library.
70. Congressional Quarterly Service, *Revolution in Civil Rights* (Washington, D.C.: Congressional Quarterly, Inc., 1965), p. 41.
71. *Weekly Compilation of Presidential Documents*, July 29, 1968, p. 1155.
72. *Public Papers of the President, 1963-1964*, II, 1669.
73. *Presidential Power: The Politics of Leadership* (New York: John Wiley & Sons, Inc., 1960).

CHAPTER III

1. *Eleventh Report of the United States Civil Service Commission, July 1, 1893 to June 30, 1894* (1895), p. 321.
2. Memorandum for the Files, April 1, 1947, Nash Files, Harry S. Truman Library.
3. *New York Times*, December 4, 1951, 26:2.
4. *The Constitution of the United States of America: Analysis and Interpretation*, Senate Document 39, 88th Cong., 1st Sess., 1963, pp. 542-553.
5. Government Contract Committee, *Sixth Report to President Eisenhower* [1959], p. 6.
6. AP news release, July 1, 1965.
7. "Analysis of the President's Mail on F.E.P.C.," OF 40, Truman Papers, Harry S. Truman Library.
8. *Congressional Quarterly Almanac*, XVI (1960), 197.
9. *Cong. Rec.*, 86th Cong., 2d Sess., 1960, CVI, 7165.
10. House Judiciary Committee, *Civil Rights Act of 1963: Report to Accompany H. R. 7152*, House Report 914, 88th Cong., 1st Sess., 1963, pt. 2, pp. 45-46, 61-64, 95, 115.
11. Malcolm Ross, *All Manner of Men* (New York: Reynal & Hitchcock, 1948), p. 21.
12. Herbert Garfinkel, *When Negroes March: The March on Washington Movement in the Organizational Politics for FEPC* (Glencoe, Ill.: The Free Press, 1959), p. 34.
13. *Ibid.*, p. 26.
14. *Ibid.*, pp. 38-42, 50.
15. Lester B. Granger, "Barriers to Negro War Employment," *Annals of the American Academy of Political and Social Science*, CCXXIII (September, 1942), 78.
16. Louis Ruchames, *Race, Jobs, & Politics: The Story of FEPC* (New York: Columbia University Press, 1953), pp. 17-18.
17. Garfinkel, *op. cit.*, p. 42.
18. Ruchames, *op. cit.*, p. 18.
19. *Ibid.*, pp. 19-20.
20. *Ibid.*, 20-21; Kesselman, *op. cit.*, p. 14.
21. John Beecher, "8802 Blues," *New Republic*, CVIII (February 22, 1943), 250.
22. *Ibid.*
23. Ruchames, *op. cit.*, p. 47.
24. Beecher, *loc. cit.*
25. Garfinkel, *op. cit.*, pp. 78-79.
26. Ruchames, *op. cit.*, pp. 47-48.
27. Ross, *op. cit.*, p. 22.
28. Florence Murray (ed.), *The Negro Handbook, 1944* (New York: Current Reference Publications), p. 212.
29. Ruchames, *op. cit.*, pp. 54-55.
30. *Cong. Rec.*, 79th Cong., 1st Sess., 1945, XCI, 5796.
31. Memorandum, Committee on Fair Employment Practice to the President, December 17, 1945, OF 40, Truman Papers, Harry S. Truman Library.
32. Memorandum, S.I.R. to the President, December 3, 1945, OF 40, Truman Papers, Harry S. Truman Library.
33. "Letter to Heads of All Government Departments, Agencies and Independent Establishments," December 18, 1945, OF 40, Truman Papers, Harry S. Truman Library.
34. Memorandum, Dawson to Clifford, March 8, 1948, OF 596, Truman Papers, Harry S. Truman Library.
35. Memorandum, Nash to Murphy, February 10, 1948, Nash Files, Harry S. Truman Library.
36. Memorandum, Charles S. Murphy to the President, December 1, 1951, OF 526-B, Truman Papers, Harry S. Truman Library.
37. Memorandum, Stephen J. Spingarn to Clark Clifford, December 19, 1949, OF 596, Truman Papers, Harry S. Truman Library.
38. Letter, Walter White to Charles E. Wilson, January 4, 1951, Nash Files, Harry S. Truman Library.
39. Memorandum, George L. P. Weaver to W. Stuart Symington, December 1, 1950, Nash Files, Harry S. Truman Library.

40. *Ibid.*
41. Letter, Attorney General J. Howard McGrath to the President, December 1, 1951, OF 526-B, Truman Papers, Harry S. Truman Library.
42. Dwight D. Eisenhower, *The White House Years: Mandate for Change* (Garden City, N.Y.: Doubleday & Company, Inc., 1963), p. 234.
43. "The President's News Conference," March 3, 1954, and "Remarks at Conference of the National Association for the Advancement of Colored People," March 10, 1954, *Public Papers of the Presidents, 1954,* pp. 293, 311.
44. Memorandum, Charles F. Willis, Jr. to Governor Adams, February 13, 1953, OF 102-I-2, Eisenhower Papers, Dwight D. Eisenhower Library.
45. Memorandums, Max Rabb to Governor Adams, April 8, 1953; Charles F. Willis, Jr. to Governor Adams, February 13, 1953; "The President's Committee on Government Contract Compliance," all in OF 102-I, Eisenhower Papers, Dwight D. Eisenhower Library.
46. According to Richard M. Nixon, quoted in the *New York Times,* August 20, 1953, 1:2.
47. Memorandums, Maxwell Rabb to Ann Whitman, July 24, 1954, OF 142-A; Maxwell Rabb to Sherman Adams, August 8, 1955, OF 142-A-4; E. Frederic Morrow to Sherman Adams, December 16, 1955, Morrow Files, all in Eisenhower Papers, Dwight D. Eisenhower Library.
48. Letter, Clarence Mitchell [Director of the Washington Bureau of the NAACP] to Maxwell Rabb, April 2, 1953, OF 102-I-1; Memorandum, Max Rabb to Governor Adams, September 20, 1954, OF 103-U, both in Eisenhower Papers, Dwight D. Eisenhower Library.
49. Memorandum, Max Rabb to Governor Adams, September 20, 1954, OF 103-U, Eisenhower Papers, Dwight D. Eisenhower Library.
50. Sherman Adams, *Firsthand Report: The Story of the Eisenhower Administration* (New York: Harper & Brothers, 1961), p. 336.
51. Eisenhower, *Mandate for Change,* p. 192.
52. Dwight D. Eisenhower, *The White House Years: Waging Peace, 1956-1961* (Garden City, N.Y.: Doubleday & Company, Inc., 1965), p. 153.
53. J. W. Anderson, *Eisenhower, Brownell, and the Congress: The Tangled Origins of the Civil Rights Bill of 1956–1957* (University, Ala.: University of Alabama Press, 1964), *passim.;* Adams, *op. cit.,* p. 335.
54. *Cong. Rec.,* 86th Cong., 2d Sess., 1960, CVI, 7165.
55. "Radio and Television Report to the American People on Civil Rights," June 11, 1963, *Public Papers of the Presidents, 1963,* p. 469.
56. Senate Labor and Public Welfare Committee, Subcommittee on Employment and Manpower, *Equal Employment Opportunity: Hearings on S. 773, S. 1210, S. 1211, and S. 1937,* 88th Cong., 1st Sess., 1963, p. 96.
57. *Congressional Quarterly Almanac,* XVII (1961), 392; Charles Lam Markmann and Mark Sherwin, *John F. Kennedy: A Sense of Purpose* (New York: St. Martin's Press, 1961), pp. 329-330.
58. *Congressional Quarterly Almanac,* XVII (1961), 392.
59. *Weekly Compilation of Presidential Documents,* September 27, 1965, pp. 302-305.
60. President's Committee on Government Contracts, "Report of Meeting with Compliance Officers," May 1, 1957, Mitchell Files, Dwight D. Eisenhower Library.
61. Fair Employment Practice Committee, *Final Report,* (1947), p. 2. The following account is based mainly on the *Final Report.*
62. President's Committee on Fair Employment Practice, "Report to the President," August 27, 1945, OF 40, Truman Papers, Harry S. Truman Library.
63. Malcolm Ross, *op. cit.,* pp. 132-133.
64. *Prohibiting Discrimination in Employment: Report and Minority Views to Accompany S. 984,* Senate Report 951, 80th Cong., 2d Sess., 1948, pt. 1, p. 2; *Federal Fair Employment Practice Act: Report to Accompany H.R.4453,* House Report 1165, 81st Cong., 1st Sess., 1949, p. 2.
65. Fair Employment Board, *First Report* (unpublished), September 30, 1949, OF "2F," Truman Papers, Harry S. Truman Library.
66. Letter, Clarence Mitchell to James L. Houghteling, November 2, 1949, and Memorandum, David K. Niles to Donald Dawson, December 12, 1950, both in OF "2F,"

Truman Papers, Harry S. Truman Library.

67. Memorandum, R. P. A. to Steelman, May 27, 1952, OF "2F," Truman Papers, Harry S. Truman Library.

68. Senate Labor and Public Welfare Committee, Subcommittee on Labor and Labor Management Relations, *Discrimination and Full Utilization of Manpower Resources: Hearings on S. 1732 and S. 651*, 82d Cong., 2d Sess., 1952, 75.

69. Memorandum, Nash to Dawson, October 5, 1951, Nash Files, Harry S. Truman Library.

70. Letter, Maxwell Abbell to Maxwell Rabb, September 16, 1955, OF 103-U, Eisenhower Papers, Dwight D. Eisenhower Library.

71. Note (initial illegible) to Mr. D. (undated), OF "2F," Truman Papers; Memorandum, M. L. F. to Mr. Dawson, December 11, 1951, "CSC-Fair Employment Board" Folder, Friedman Files, Harry S. Truman Library.

72. President's Committee on Government Employment Policy, *Fourth Report*, 1961, pp. 23-24.

73. Memorandum, Maxwell M. Rabb to the President, June 6, 1956, OF 103-U, Eisenhower Papers, Dwight D. Eisenhower Library.

74. *Report, 1961*, Bk. 3, p. 37.

75. *Ibid.*, pp. 69-70. See Government Contract Committee, *Fourth Annual Report on Equal Job Opportunity*, 1957, pp. 9, 15-16.

76. Letter, Jacob Seidenberg [Executive Director] to James P. Mitchell [vice chairman], December 27, 1959; Note (undated), Sherman Adams to Mr. Mitchell; Letter, Helen Reid [Committee member] to James P. Mitchell, March 4, 1960; and Note (undated), Maxwell Hamilton [consultant] to Walter C. Wallace [Executive Assistant to Secretary Mitchell], all in Mitchell Files, Harry S. Truman Library.

77. President's Committee on Equal Employment Opportunity, *Report to the President*, November 26, 1963, pp. 1, 28.

78. *Ibid.*, p. 3.

79. "Remarks to Participants in the Signing of Equal Opportunity Agreements," June 22, 1962, *Public Papers of the Presidents, 1962*, p. 506; "Special Message to the Congress on Civil Rights," February 28, 1963, *Ibid.*, 1963, p. 228.

80. President's Committee on Equal Employment Opportunity, *op. cit.*, p. 4.

81. *Ibid.*, p. 108.

82. *Equal Employment Opportunity: Hearings on S. 773, S. 1210, S. 1211, and S. 1937*, p. 391.

83. *Ibid.*; "Special Message to the Congress on Civil Rights," February 28, 1963, *Public Papers of the Presidents, 1963*, p. 227.

84. These statements and requests are included in *Public Papers of the Presidents, 1963*, *passim.*

85. *New York Times*, April 8, 1961, 1:1; *Equal Employment Opportunity: Hearings on S. 773, S. 1210, S. 1211, and S. 1937*, p. 163.

86. *Op. cit.*, pp. 132-133.

87. *Equal Employment Opportunity: Hearings on S. 773, S. 1210, S. 1211, and S. 1937*, p. 481.

88. House Education and Labor Committee, Special Subcommittee on Labor, *Hearings on Equal Employment Opportunity*, 87th Cong., 1st Sess., 1961, pt. 1, p. 175.

CHAPTER IV

1. Bk. 4, p. 140.

2. Quoted in Letter, Arthur B. Spingarn, Walter White, Louis T. Wright to Harry S. Truman, September 25, 1951, Nash Files, Harry S. Truman Library.

3. National Housing Agency, Racial Relations Service, *Minority Group Considerations in Administration of Government Housing Program*, July 11, 1947. [Mimeo.], Records of President's Committee on Civil Rights, Harry S. Truman Library.

4. U.S. Commission on Civil Rights, *Report, 1961*, Bk. 4, p. 24. See National Association for the Advancement of Colored People, *Memorandum Covering the Present Discriminatory Policies of the Federal Housing Administration*, October 28, 1944, [Mimeo.], copy in Records of President's Committee on Civil Rights, Harry S.

Truman Library.

5. Memorandum, November 15, 1946, as quoted in *Minority Group Considerations in Administration of Governmental Housing Programs.*

6. "Statement by Solicitor General Philip B. Perlman at Luncheon Session of State-wide Conference of New York State Committee on Discrimination in Housing," copy of news release in Spingarn Papers, Harry S. Truman Library.

7. Memorandum, Philleo Nash to Donald S. Dawson, June 16, 1952, Nash Files, Harry S. Truman Library.

8. In *Cong. Rec.,* 81st Cong., 1st Sess., 1949, XCV, 8658.

9. "Statement by the President on Equal Opportunity in Housing," April 12, 1962, *Public Papers of the Presidents of the United States: John F. Kennedy, 1962* (Washington: Government Printing Office, 1963), p. 324. Hereafter cited as *Public Papers of the Presidents.*

10. Letters, Abraham J. Multer to Harry S. Truman, April 24, 1951; Arthur B. Spingarn, Walter White, Louis T. Wright to Harry S. Truman, September 25, 1951; Walter White to Philleo Nash, October 16, 1961; J. K. Javits to Harry S. Truman, October 26, 1951; all in the Nash Files, Harry S. Truman Library.

11. *To Secure These Rights: The Report of the President's Committee on Civil Rights* (New York: Simon & Schuster, 1947), p. 166.

12. "Suggested Outline of Omnibus Civil Rights Bill of 1948," Spingarn Papers, Harry S. Truman Library.

13. Memorandum, Philleo Nash to Charles S. Murphy, September 20, 1951, Nash Files, Harry S. Truman Library.

14. Letter from American Council on Human Rights to Dwight D. Eisenhower, March 14, 1953, GF 124-A-5, Eisenhower Papers, Dwight D. Eisenhower Library.

15. Memorandum, Maxwell Rabb to Sherman Adams, July 15, 1954, OF 120, Eisenhower Papers, Dwight D. Eisenhower Library.

16. Memorandum, Maxwell Rabb to Sherman Adams, July 16, 1954, OF 120, Eisenhower Papers, Dwight D. Eisenhower Library.

17. See news conferences of August 5, 1954, and February 4, 1959, in *Public Papers of the Presidents.*

18. *Trends in Housing,* VI (September–October, 1962), 3.

19. "Proposed Executive Order Relating to Equal Opportunity in Housing," OF 120, Eisenhower Papers, Dwight D. Eisenhower Library.

20. Note (undated) initialed DWK (David W. Kendall, Special Counsel to the President) relating telephone conversation on January 13, 1960, with Norman Mason, OF 120, Eisenhower Papers, Dwight D. Eisenhower Library.

21. U.S. Commission on Civil Rights, *Hearings on Housing,* 1959, I, 365.

22. *Ibid.,* p. 337.

23. *Trends in Housing,* VI (September–October, 1962), 4.

24. *Cong. Rec.,* 87th Cong., 2d Sess., 1962, CVIII, 20303-20304.

25. U.S. Commission on Civil Rights, *Report, 1961,* Bk. 4, pp. 67, 71, 101.

26. Charles Abrams, *Forbidden Neighbors: A Study of Prejudice in Housing* (New York: Harper & Brothers, 1955), p. 154; *Cong. Rec.,* 81st Cong., 1st Sess., 1949, XCV, 4853.

27. *Cong. Rec.,* 81st Cong., 1st Sess., 1949, XCV, 4854.

28. *Ibid.*

29. Letter, Abraham J. Multer to Harry S. Truman, August 24, 1951, Nash Files, Harry S. Truman Library.

30. *Ibid.*

31. Memorandum, Philleo Nash to Donald S. Dawson, June 16, 1952, Nash Files, Harry S. Truman Library

32. In Nash Files, Harry S. Truman Library.

33. Letter, Raymond M. Foley to Abraham J. Multer, November 26, 1951, Nash Files, Harry S. Truman Library.

34. *Housing Authority of City and County of San Francisco* v. *Mattie Banks,* 120 Cal. App. 2d 1,260 P. 2d 668 (1953), cert. denied 347 U.S. 974 (1954.)

35. Senator Sparkman, *Cong. Rec.,* 87th Cong., 2d Sess., 1962, CVIII, 22908. See James E. Palmer, Jr., "An Analysis of the Authority of the President to Issue an Executive

Order Concerning Racial Integration in Federal Housing Programs," reprinted on pp. 22908-22912.
36. Theodore C. Sorensen, *Kennedy* (New York: Harper & Row Publishers, 1965), p. 480.
37. *Ibid.*
38. *Ibid.*
39. Arthur M. Schlesinger, Jr., *A Thousand Days: John F. Kennedy in the White House* (Boston: Houghton Mifflin Company, 1965), p. 939.
40. Sorensen, *op. cit.*, p. 481.
41. *Ibid.*
42. *New York Times*, November 27, 1961, 22:3; Sorensen, *op. cit.*, p. 481
43. Sorensen, *op. cit.*, p. 481.
44. *Ibid.*, pp. 481-482.
45. Martin E. Sloane, "One Year's Experience: Current and Potential Impact of the Housing Order," *The George Washington Law Review*, XXXII (March, 1964), 459.
46. Senator John J. Sparkman, *Cong. Rec.*, 87th Cong., 2d Sess., 1962, CVIII, 22908.
47. *New York Times*, November 21, 1962, 19:1.
48. Sorensen, *op. cit.*, p. 483; *Trends in Housing*, VI (September-October, 1962), 4.
49. *Op. cit.*, pp. 480, 482.
50. Martin E. Sloane and Monroe H. Freedman, "The Executive Order on Housing: The Constitutional Basis for What It Fails to Do," *Howard Law Journal*, IX (Winter, 1963), 1-19.
51. *U.S. News & World Report*, LIII (September 17, 1962), 46.
52. *New York Times*, November 21, 1962, 19:3.
53. *Ibid.*, November 22, 1962, 32:1.
54. National Committee Against Discrimination in Housing, *Equal Opportunity in Housing: Challenge To American Communities* (1963), p. 7. Hereafter cited as *Report on 1963 Housing Conference*.
55. *New York Times*, November 21, 1962, 19:3.
56. *Report on 1963 Housing Conference*, p. 7; *Trends in Housing*, VI (September-October, 1962), 3.
57. *U.S. News & World Report*, LIII (September 17, 1962), 46.
58. *Trends in Housing*, VI (September-October, 1962), 4.
59. *Report on 1963 Housing Conference*, p. 30.
60. Senator Herman Talmadge, *Trends in Housing*, VI (September-October, 1962), 3; National Association of Home Builders, *ibid.*; Senator A. Willis Robertson, *New York Times*, November 21, 1962, 19:2.
61. Senator John Stennis, *New York Times*, November 21, 1962, 19:2.
62. Consult Arthur Krock's column in *New York Times*, November 23, 1962, 28:3.
63. Charles J. Bloch, "Property Rights—Are There Any?" *North Carolina Law Review*, XLII (1963), 136-153; Milton P. Semer and Martin E. Sloane, "Equal Housing Opportunity and Individual Property Rights," *The Federal Bar Journal*, XXIV (Winter, 1964), 47-75.
64. Semer and Sloane, *loc. cit.*, p. 48.
65. *New York Times*, November 22, 1962, 32:1.
66. *Report on 1963 Housing Conference*, pp. 1-3.
67. *Ibid.*, p. 6.
68. *Ibid.*
69. U.S. Commission on Civil Rights, *Report, 1963*, p. 99, n. 10.
70. Sorensen, *op. cit.*, p. 497; see "Special Message to the Congress on Civil Rights and Job Opportunities," June 19, 1963, *Public Papers of the Presidents, 1963*, p. 492.
71. "Candidate John Kennedy Discusses the Presidency," in Donald Bruce Johnson and Jack C. Walker (eds.) *The Dynamics of the American Presidency* (New York: John Wiley & Sons, Inc., 1964), pp. 139-141.
72. Schlesinger, *op. cit.*, p. 928.

CHAPTER V

1. The familiar definition of politics is David Easton's. See his book *The Political System* (New York: Alfred A. Knopf, 1953), pp. 129-134.
2. Memorandum, Maxwell M. Rabb to Governor Adams, July 8, 1953, OF 102-I-2, Eisenhower Papers, Dwight D. Eisenhower Library.
3. Memorandum, Max Rabb to Mr. Willis, September 17, 1954, OF 103-U, Eisenhower Papers, Dwight D. Eisenhower Library.
4. Memorandum, Sherman Adams to Attorney General, April 14, 1953, OF 102-I-1, Eisenhower Papers, Dwight D. Eisenhower Library.

Bibliography

The literature on the President and on civil rights is so extensive that the following sources can only be considered as samples. They are arranged according to the main topics of this study.

THE PRESIDENT

The best textbook teatment is Louis W. Koenig, *The Chief Executive* (New York: Harcourt, Brace & World, Inc., 1964); the most succinct overview is Clinton Rossiter, *The American Presidency* (New York: Harcourt, Brace & Company, 1956); and the most detailed general work is Joseph E. Kallenbach, *The American Chief Executive: The Presidency and the Governorship* (New York: Harper & Row, Publishers, 1966). More interpretive is Richard E. Neustadt, *Presidential Power: The Politics of Leadership* (New York: John Wiley & Sons, Inc., [1960]).

Still a basic reference on the constitutional aspects of the Presidency is Edward S. Corwin, *The President: Office and Powers, 1787–1957* (4th rev. ed., New York: New York University Press, 1957). A valuable aid to the study of the constitutional powers of the President is *The Constitution of the United States of America: Analysis and Interpretation* (88th Congress, 1st Session, Senate Document No. 39, 1964).

For important specialized studies, see Glendon A. Schubert, *The Presidency in the Courts* (Minneapolis: University of Minnesota Press, 1957); Wilfred E. Binkley, *The President and Congress* (3d rev. ed., New York: Vintage Books,

1962), for a historical treatment; Lawrence H. Chamberlain, *The President, Congress and Legislation* (New York: Columbia University Press, 1946), for an analysis of the relative influence of Congress and the President on legislation; and Elmer E. Cornwell, Jr., *Presidential Leadership of Public Opinion* (Bloomington: Indiana University Press, 1965), for a study of the President's relation to the public.

Richard Longaker examines the President's responsibility to protect individual liberty in *The President and Civil Liberties* (Ithaca, N.Y.: Cornell University Press, 1961). Also see his "The President and the Civil Rights of Negroes," *American Government Annual, 1962–1963* (New York: Holt, Rinehart and Winston, Inc., 1962), pp. 53–69.

Valuable information can be found in the memoirs and papers of the Presidents. The Truman memoirs are published in two volumes as *Year of Decision* and *Years of Trial and Hope* (Garden City, N.Y.: Doubleday & Company, Inc., 1955, 1956), and the Eisenhower memoirs in two volumes as *The White House Years* (Garden City, N.Y.: Doubleday & Company, Inc., 1963, 1965).

The published papers of Roosevelt are available in Samuel I. Rosenman (comp.), *The Public Papers and Addresses of Franklin D. Roosevelt* (9 Vols., New York: Random House, 1938). In 1957 the U.S. government began publishing an official series, *The Public Papers of the Presidents of the United States.* Volumes are available covering the administrations of Presidents Truman, Eisenhower, Kennedy, and Johnson.

POLICY-MAKING

Many recent books acknowledge the expansion of Presidential policy-making functions. See Charles E. Lindblom, *The Policy-Making Process* (Englewood Cliffs, N.J.: Prentice-Hall, Inc., 1968). For an excellent discussion of incremental politics, see David Braybrooke and Charles E. Lindblom, *A Strategy of Decision: Policy Evaluation as a Social Process* (New York: The Free Press of Glencoe, 1963), especially Part II. For an analysis of the environment of policy-making, consult Louis W. Koenig, *Congress and the President* (Chicago: Scott, Foresman and Company, 1965), pp. 5–15, 152–153.

A short, readable book on Presidential decision-making is Theodore C. Sorensen, *Decision-Making in the White House: The Olive Branch or the Arrows* (New York: Columbia University Press, 1963). Thomas E. Cronin and Sanford D. Greenberg have edited an excellent anthology on *The Presidential Advisory System* (New York: Harper & Row, Publishers, 1969).

An ambitious attempt to identify the variables that affect Presidential decision-making is the work of Richard C. Snyder and his colleagues, and Glenn D. Paige. The original formulation of Snyder's decision-making schema is conveniently reprinted in Richard C. Snyder, H. W. Bruck, and Burton Sapin (eds.), *Foreign Policy Decision Making: An Approach to the Study of International Politics* (New York: The Free Press, 1962), pp. 14–185. For an application, see Glenn D. Paige, *The Korean Decision* (New York: The Free Press, 1968).

EXECUTIVE ORDERS

Little has been written specifically about the Executive order. The only book that deals at any length with aspects of the subject is *The Ordinance*

Making Powers of the President of the United States by James Hart (Baltimore: The Johns Hopkins Press, 1925). For a comparison with the ordinance making power in English and French law, see Marguerite A. Sieghart, *Government by Decree: A Comparative Study of the History of the Ordinance in English and French Law* (London: Stevens & Sons Ltd., 1950).

In 1944 the Senate authorized the Committee on the Judiciary to survey and report the constitutional or statutory authority upon which Executive orders issued by the President after March 4, 1933, were based. The only report this study produced was the *Report on Executive Order 9438 (Montgomery Ward & Co., Inc.)* (Confidential Committee Print, 78th Congress, 2d Session, 1944). In 1957 a study was made for the U.S. House Committee on Government Operations on *Executive Orders and Proclamations: A Study of a Use of Presidential Powers* (Committee Print, 85th Congress, 1st Session, 1957).

The texts of Executive orders issued after 1935 are available in the *Federal Register,* and are compiled in Title 3 of the *Code of Federal Regulations.* Lists of Executive orders issued prior to the publication of the *Federal Register* are available. See U.S. Works Projects Administration, Historical Records Survey, *Presidential Executive Orders* (2 vols. [New York]: Hastings House, 1944) for the numbered series, and Clifford L. Lord (ed.), *List and Index of Presidential Executive Orders (Unnumbered Series) 1789–1941* (Newark, N.J.: The New Jersey Historical Records Survey, Works Projects Administration, 1943) [Mimeographed].

CIVIL RIGHTS

Works that provide helpful background on this subject include W. J. Cash, *The Mind of the South* (New York: A. A. Knopf, 1941); Eli Ginzberg, *The Negro Potential* (New York: Columbia University Press, 1956), and Gunnar Myrdahl, *An American Dilemma: The Negro Problem and Modern Democracy* (New York: Harper and Brothers, Publishers, 1944).

For an account of the struggle for civil rights, 1954–1964, compiled from daily reports in the *New York Times* and Sunday *Times* magazine articles, see Anthony Lewis and the *New York Times, Portrait of a Decade: The Second American Revolution* (New York: Random House, 1964). Also helpful is Jacob K. Javits, *Discrimination—USA* (New York: Harcourt, Brace & Company, 1960).

C. Van Woodward gives a historical account of Jim Crow laws in *The Strange Career of Jim Crow* (New York: Oxford, 1955). Good sources for the law of race relations are Jack Greenberg, *Race Relations and American Law* (New York: Columbia University, 1959), and Morroe Berger, *Equality by Statute: Legal Controls over Group Discrimination* (New York: Columbia University Press, 1952). For an analysis of the constitutional aspects of the struggle for civil rights, see Milton R. Konvitz and Theodore Leskes, *A Century of Civil Rights with a Study of State Law against Discrimination* (New York: Columbia University Press, 1961). The Congressional Quarterly Service's *Revolution in Civil Rights* (4th ed., Washington, 1968) is a good source for the legislative histories of civil rights bills.

Excellent studies of the role of Congress and of the judicial branch of the government in civil rights matters are available. J. W. Anderson gives a detailed account of the unsuccessful efforts to pass the 1956 Civil Rights Bill in *Eisen-*

hower, Brownell, and the Congress: The Tangled Origins of the Civil Rights Bill of 1956-1957 (University, Ala.: University of Alabama Press, 1964). Daniel M. Berman examines the history of the Civil Rights Acts of 1960 and 1964 in *A Bill Becomes A Law: Congress Enacts Civil Rights Legislation* (2d ed., New York: The Macmillan Company, 1966). Descriptions of the enactment and implementation of state and local antidiscrimination laws are contained in *Toward Equal Opportunity: A Study of State and Local Antidiscrimination Laws* (New York: The Macmillan Company, 1968).

Clement E. Vose describes the events leading to the decisions in the Restrictive Covenant Cases of 1948 and 1953 in *Caucasians Only: The Supreme Court, the NAACP, and the Restrictive Covenant Cases* (Berkeley: University of California Press, 1959). Daniel M. Berman discusses the School Segregation Cases in *It Is So Ordered: The Supreme Court Rules on School Segregation* (New York: W. W. Norton & Co., Inc., 1966). An interesting account of the role of the federal judges in the circuit and district courts of the South in carrying out the decisions of the U.S. Supreme Court against segregation can be found in J. W. Peltason's *Fifty-Eight Lonely Men: Southern Federal Judges and School Desegregation* (New York: Harcourt, Brace & World, Inc., 1961).

Valuable government document sources include the President's Committee on Civil Rights, *To Secure These Rights* (1947); the White House Conference "To Fulfill These Rights, *Report* (1966), the U.S. Commission on Civil Rights, *Freedom to the Free: Century of Emancipation* (1963); and the many other reports issued by the U.S. Commission on Civil Rights since 1959. Other good sources of information are the reports and the hearings on civil rights bills of the House and Senate Committees on the Judiciary and the House Rules Committee.

MILITARY DESEGREGATION

Discussions of the efforts to desegregate the military can be found in Langston Hughes, *Fight for Freedom: The Story of the NAACP* (New York: W. W. Norton & Company, Inc., 1962); Lee Nichols, *Breakthrough on the Color Front* (New York: Random House, 1954); and Walter White, *How Far the Promised Land?* (New York: The Viking Press, 1955) and also his autobiography, *A Man Called White* (New York: The Viking Press, 1948). A good reference is Dennis D. Nelson, *The Integration of the Negro into the U.S. Army* (New York: Farrar, Straus & Young, 1951). A case study of the Selective Service Act of 1948 that includes an account of the controversy over civil rights amendments is Clyde E. Jacobs and John F. Gallagher, *The Selective Service Act: A Case Study of the Governmental Process* (New York: Dodd, Mead & Company, 1967).

Government document sources include the report of the President's Committee on Equality of Treatment and Opportunity in the Armed Services, *Freedom to Serve* (1950), and the hearings of the Senate and House Armed Services Committees.

FAIR EMPLOYMENT PRACTICES

For a history of the wartime experience with FEPC, consult Herbert Garfinkel, *When Negroes March* (Glencoe, Ill.: The Free Press, 1959); Malcolm Ross, *All Manner of Men* (New York: Reynal & Hitchcock, 1948), and Louis

Ruchames, *Race, Jobs, & Politics: The Story of FEPC* (New York: Columbia University Press, 1953). An important study of the movement for a permanent national Fair Employment Practice Commission is Louis Kesselman, *The Social Politics of FEPC: A Study in Reform Pressure Movements* (Chapel Hill: The University of North Carolina Press, 1948). For an appraisal of the administration of federal, state, and local fair employment practices programs, see *Toward Fair Employment* by Paul H. Norgren and Samuel E. Hill (New York: Columbia University Press, 1964).

Studies of the Negro in government employment include Laurence J. W. Hayes, *The Negro Federal Government Worker* (Washington: Howard University, 1941) and Samuel Krislov, *The Negro in Federal Employment* (Minneapolis: University of Minnesota Press, 1967). Good for background on this subject is Paul P. Van Riper, *History of the United States Civil Service* (Evanston, Ill.: Row, Peterson and Company, 1958).

The U.S. government document sources include the reports of the Civil Service Commission, the reports of the various Presidential committees dealing with fair employment practices, and the reports and hearings of the Senate Labor and Public Welfare Committee and the House Education and Labor Committee. Of the reports issued by the U.S. Commission on Civil Rights, Book III of the 1961 *Report* is especially helpful.

FAIR HOUSING

General background information can be found in the report of the Commission on Race and Housing, *Where Shall We Live?* (Berkeley: University of California Press, 1958), and in *Forbidden Neighbors: A Study of Prejudice in Housing* by Charles Abrams (New York: Harper & Brothers, 1955). Much valuable information is contained in *Trends in Housing,* published bimonthly since August, 1956, by the National Committee Against Discrimination in Housing.

For government document sources, consult the publications of the Housing and Home Finance Agency and the U.S. Commission on Civil Rights. Particularly helpful are Housing and Home Finance Agency, Public Housing Administration, *Equal Opportunity in Housing, Series of Case Studies* (June, 1964), and the U.S. Commission on Civil Rights, *Hearings on Housing* (2 vols., 1959) and Book IV of *Report, 1961.*

Index